DATE DUE

GARLAND STUDIES ON THE ELDERLY IN AMERICA

edited by
STUART BRUCHEY
University of Maine

A GARLAND SERIES

MARRIED WIDOWS

WIVES OF MEN IN LONG-TERM CARE

MARIA C. BARTLETT

GARLAND PUBLISHING, INC.
NEW YORK & LONDON / 1993

Library of Congress Cataloging-in-Publication Data

Bartlett, Maria C., 1946–
    Married widows : wives of men in long-term care / Maria C. Bartlett.
        p.   cm. — (Garland studies on the elderly in America)
    Includes bibliographical references.
    ISBN 0–8153–1535–X (alk. paper)
    1. Nursing home patients' wives—Mental health. 2. Nursing home
patients—Family relationships. I. Title. II. Series.
RC451.4.N87B37   1993
362.1'6—dc20   93–22707
                                                                      CIP

Printed on acid-free, 250-year-life paper
Manufactured in the United States of America

To my Grandparents

CONTENTS

LIST OF TABLES

PREFACE

As a hospital social worker on a geriatric service, I coordinated hundreds of nursing home placements and saw the effects on those who were caregivers. Literature on caregivers abounds but very little focuses on caregiving by families after placement. "Married widows" describes a group of wives who shared their stories about caring for husbands who were transferred to nursing homes. What happens to these women's roles and relationships? To what extent are these women vulnerable? How do they voice their needs? Throughout the interviews with 24 women, individual and universal themes emerged. Coping mechanisms included positive thinking, religion, humor and stoicism. Despite the hardships of illness and major life transitions, the wives remained committed to their institutionalized husbands. Love prevailed and was reflected in positive assessments of long-term marriages.

ACKNOWLEDGMENTS

To all of those who have inspired and sustained me throughout this endeavor, I am forever grateful. It is impossible to list individually the many people who have encouraged me and contributed in countless ways to the realization of this work.

I am very grateful to the wives who participated in this study, for sharing their personal, and sometimes painful, memories.

I am most indebted to the chair of my committee, Don Brieland, for his wisdom and wit.

I would further like to thank my committee members, Sidney Zimbalist, Marie Robinson, and William Schubert, for their valuable ideas and criticisms; Baila Miller for her contributions in the development of the design and methodology; and Nathan Linsk, who recommended me for the program and inspired my interest in the field of gerontology.

I am grateful to Natalie Seltzer for her support and encouragement. Special thanks are due to the Department of Medical Social Work, University of Illinois at Chicago, for their cooperation, patience and endurance.

Most valuable service was provided by Penny Patterson, in her enthusiastic and tireless entries and editions on the word processor.

Thanks to my family and friends for their understanding and tolerance of the many times it was necessary to decline social invitations!

A special thanks to Dr. Dan Brauner for his friendship and for being there.

Finally, I would like to express my most sincere appreciation to Peter Draper, for his affection and confidence in me throughout the project.

MCB

INTRODUCTION

"It is interesting that so much attention is devoted to the
family roles of women in the few years they are mothers of
young children and how little really is known about them in
the decades that follow, when that role recedes in salience.
Who are the husband-focused women?" (H.Z. Lopata, 1987)

In the United States, over the course of a lifetime, the risk of
nursing home placement is as high as 48% (Wingard, Jones and
Kaplan, 1987). Over 1.5 million elderly Americans reside in long-term
care facilities (Branch, 1989). As the proportion of elderly increases,
the number of nursing home residents is projected to increase
dramatically. Precipitating factors in nursing home placement include
living alone, physical frailty, mental status changes, incontinence,
frequent falls, sudden and chronic illness, and the loss of a caregiver
or spouse (Given, Collins and King, 1989).

Elderly spouses remain the predominant source of care for older
ill persons who live at home (Klein, Dean and Bogdonoff, 1967) prior
to placement (Zarit, Reever and Bach-Peterson, 1986). Literature on
family caregiving is abundant; however, few studies address the issues
of caring for a spouse after placement. Specifically, what is the impact
of placement on the marriage, and how does the husband or wife who
is not placed perceive the experience?

Men have traditionally married younger women. Men also have
a shorter life expectancy than women. They are therefore not as likely
to become widowers as women are likely to become widows, and many
men solve the problem of widowhood by remarrying (Silverman,
1986). Loss of a spouse is often a point of entry into the long-term care
system.

Although the majority of nursing home residents are widows, this
study is concerned with the effects of placement on caregivers. The
caregiver role falls most clearly on women. Therefore, this study deals
with wives whose spouses have undergone nursing home placement.

1

BACKGROUND

Women as Caregivers

The socialization of women takes place within the broad environment of time, politics and history, and the personal context of relationships with others. One's development from childhood through adulthood incorporates a span of temporal and life events. These changes, interactions, and adaptations transform one's identity. It is the process of becoming who we are.

Gilligan (1982) asserts that women's and men's psychological development differ. According to Gilligan, women evolve in terms of attachment and an "ethic of care". This ethic of care is the link between relationship and responsibility.

Characteristically, women are ascribed and assume a nurturant role. Childcare continues to be provided primarily by mothers. Daughters often become the principal caregivers to their aging parents. Neugarten (1968) found that the timing and order of major life events in women's lives is dependent on the life events faced by other family members. As Brody (1985) noted, the lifelong caretaker role of women is fundamentally dependent on the needs of others.

STATEMENT OF THE PROBLEM

The first purpose of this study was to assess the impact of nursing home placement on the wives of residents. How do these women describe their experience? How do they cope with changes in roles and relationships? The second purpose was to discover if these women were at risk and, if so, to determine both their concrete and clinical needs.

REVIEW OF LITERATURE

LONG-TERM MARRIAGES

Families continuously undergo major changes in structure as a result of processes in the family life cycle, in this case, aging. When a husband and wife are committed to staying together, they have the chance to grow old together, a romanticized concept depicted in movies (e.g., On Golden Pond) and songs (e.g., "Silver Threads Among the Gold").

Commitment appears to be important to maintaining a long-term relationship. According to a study of retired people in Norway by Swenson and Trahaug (1985), spouses committed to each other as persons, as opposed to being committed to the institution of marriage, had significantly fewer marital problems. The commitment of partners to one another as persons provides the basis for the resolution of problems. One can hypothesize that commitment offers the security that makes it possible for a couple to risk and problem-solve.

Turner (1970) has suggested that when the marital relationship incorporates more than spousal functions, the relationship is strengthened and more resilient. When this occurs, the spouse becomes irreplaceable.

Early studies suggested that marital satisfaction declined with length of marriage (Pineo, 1961; Birren et al., 1963; Cuber and Harroff, 1965). However, older couples have reported a significantly lower number of marital problems (Gilford and Bengston, 1979). There is significantly less negative sentiment in the marriages of older people. Recent research has found a curvilinear relationship between marital quality and stages in the family life cycle. The youngest and the oldest couples report higher marital quality (Anderson, Russell and Schumm, 1983).

Lewis and Spanier (1979) indicated that the primary determinant of the stability of a marriage is its quality. The qualities found in strong, long-term relationships are consistent with those identified in previous studies of family strengths (Beam, 1979; Stinnett and Sauer, 1977; Stinnett et al., 1982) and include the capacity to deal with crises in a positive manner. Research suggests that a family's ability to deal positively with crises stems from trust developed by relying on themselves. In a study of family strengths in long-term marriages by MacKinnon, MacKinnon and Franken (1984), individuals in strong, long-term relationships tended to engage in reframing to avoid passive appraisal and the need for social support. Strong families redefined stressful events to make them more manageable. They were unlikely to react passively, waiting for outside agents to resolve a problem. They held idealistic attitudes about the probability of relationship conflicts and were confident of their successful resolution. Older married couples are unlike other husbands and wives. They have had an intimate relationship for a longer period of time. They are past the pressures of raising children and earning a living. Eventually, they face the problem of accumulated losses. Friends and siblings die, and the marriage itself may be stressed by serious illness, and finally ended by death.

THE IMPACT OF ILLNESS ON THE ELDERLY SPOUSE

Illness exerts a significant effect upon the well members of a family. Most research on illness in families has focused on the patient. Far less research has looked at the impact of illness on the spouse. However, Golodetz et al., (1969), were especially sensitive in recognizing the significance of the caregiving work role of the female spouse:

> She is not trained for her job, a priori. She may have little choice about doing the job. She belongs to no union or guild, works no fixed maximum of hours. She lacks formal compensation, job advancement and even the possibility of being fired. She has no job mobility. In her work situation, she bears a heavy emotional load, but has no colleagues or supervisor or education to help her handle this. Her own life and its needs compete constantly with her work requirements. She may be limited in her performance by her own ailments. (p.390)

Three quarters of the people studied by Golodetz et al., were over 60 and more than half had significant illnesses of their own. These authors felt that wives provide a special kind of care and "commitment and sympathy that can invaluably complement professional detachment." Given this special attribute they believe the spouse is often as needy as the patient and that attention must be given the wife as well.

In a study of wives of elderly disabled men, Fengler and Goodrich (1979) found that wives may be suddenly called upon to accept responsibilities that their husbands are unable to fulfill. They become family breadwinners, carry out new domestic chores, and make major decisions in areas formerly assumed by their husbands.

Waltz (1986) investigated the marital context of quality of life of post-infarct patients. He suggested that there is an over-emphasis of the concept of social support as a buffer of stress and that the identification of love resources related to positive feeling states and life satisfaction has not received the attention it deserves. A pivotal aspect of any major psychosocial transition in people's lives is the alteration of the self-concept. A high level of life satisfaction prior to illness and mutual obligation in marriage provide the prerequisites Waltz ascribes for mastering adaptive tasks.

ABUSE

A certain amount of violence in the family is often tolerated as "normal" in the sense that it is deserved. An example is abuse exchanged among siblings. Despite the fact that family violence is prevalent, the family is still potentially the most nurturing source of support for its members, especially its elders.

The data on abuse cites the stresses of caregiving as a major factor in cases of violence against the elderly (O'Malley et al., 1983). Most of this research has focused on adults who abuse parents because of the stress of caregiving. Very little research has dealt with elderly spouse abuse.

Definition of Abuse

What is abuse and how is it defined? One of the difficulties which plagues the literature is the lack of consensus regarding what constitutes abuse. Methods, findings, and subsequent recommendations therefore, are not consistent.

In general, abuse refers to improper treatment, abusive language or physical maltreatment. Clearly, abuse can refer to physical assault, verbal threats, maltreatment, and sexual violence, as well as financial, psychological and self-abuse. Wife abuse has become a political rather than a scientific term as it is rarely defined so that it can be measured "objectively".

Identification and Prevalence of Elder Abuse

Literature on abuse has focused on children and younger wives. The problem of elder abuse has been reported as affecting only "small numbers" of older people (Callahan, 1988).

In the first large scale random survey involving over 2,000 elderly in the Boston area, the prevalence of overall maltreatment was 32 elderly per 1000 (Pillemer and Finklehor, 1988). Spouses were the most likely abusers, with roughly equal numbers of men and women as victims. In a smaller study, Pillemer (1985) found an "interesting variant" of five cases of elderly wives who identified their sick and dependent husbands as abusive.

Two preliminary attempts to estimate the prevalence of elder abuse in the population have both conceptual and methodological problems. Block and Sinott (1979) found an elderly abuse rate of 4%. However, the response rate was only 16%, and the final sample size only 73. Both sample size and lack of definition of abuse render the findings ungeneralizable.

Gioglio and Blakemore (1983) sampled 342 elders in New Jersey and found that only five reported some form of maltreatment. This study used volunteer interviewers and somewhat vague measures of abuse.

To date, only five studies have described a series of ten or more cases of abuse of elderly institutionalized persons (O'Malley, Segal and Perez, 1979; Block and Sinott, 1979; Douglas, Hickey and Noel, 1980; Steurer and Austin, 1980; Lau and Kosberg, 1979). All differ widely in their definitions and methodology. Several of these studies gained information from the response of health care providers to mail surveys or personal interviews (O'Malley, Segal and Perez, 1979; Block and Sinott, 1979; Douglas, Hickey and Noel, 1980). Two studies were based on retrospective chart reviews (Steurer and Austin, 1980; Lau and Kosberg, 1979). These studies found that victims were predominantly old and female. However, references to causation and intervention were few.

Theories of Cause

Although the literature has presented little evidence on the causes of elder abuse, four primary theories emphasize different elements:
1) The physical and mental impairment of the abused (Zarit, Reever and Bach-Peterson, 1980; Fengler and Goodrich, 1979).
2) The effect of external stresses on the abuser (the stressed caregiver).
3) Abuse as a learned behavior (Straus, 1977) (the violent family).
4) The individual problems of the abuser (the pathological abuser) (O'Rourke, 1980).
These theories imply that only separation of the abused and the abuser, or strategies to reduce or contain the abuser's behavior will reduce the abuse. Other interventions include counseling to reduce stress, support groups, respite care and supportive services.

Dependency of the victim has been proposed as a causative factor which can lead to abuse (O'Malley, Segal and Perez, 1979; Hickey and Douglas, 1981). This most often involves a dependent elderly parent and a son or daughter. The extreme care needs of the parent, coupled with the inverted relationship, frustrates the son or daughter in the caregiver role and leads to acts of abuse.

In contrast to the accepted belief that abuse of the elderly is most often perpetrated by their children, Pillemer and Finklehor (1988) found the largest proportion of elder abuse among spouses. Fifty-eight percent of the abuse found by Pillemer and Finklehor (1988) was spousal (37 cases out of 63); 23 of the abusers were wives and 14 were husbands. Two other unpublished reports also concluded that spouse abuse was the more prevalent form (Hageboeck and Brandt, 1981; Giordano, 1982). Finklehor (1983) noted that abuse can occur as a response to powerlessness. Pillemer (1985) hypothesized that a dependent abuser responds to his or her lack of power in the relationship by abusing the caregiver. In these studies of elderly spouse abuse it is not known if the victim was also in the dependent role within the marital dyad.

Demographics

Studies of violence in the elderly population yielded several demographic conclusions. Previous studies demonstrated that elder abuse victims came predominantly from disadvantaged segments of the population (Hudson, 1986; Johnson, 1985). In contrast to studies by Hudson (1986) and Johnson (1985), Pillemer and Finklehor (1988) found no relationships with race, economics or education. The abused elderly victims did not come from disadvantaged segments of the population.

O'Malley, Segal and Perez, (1979), and Wolf, Godkin and Pillemer (1984), found that abused elders were more likely to be living with someone else. Pillemer and Finklehor (1988) also reported that elderly persons living with a spouse and one other person were particularly vulnerable to abuse. According to Lau and Kosberg (1979) and Pillemer and Finklehor (1988) abused elderly were more likely to be in poor health.

Gender

Contrary to public opinion, Pillemer and Finklehor (1988) found that more males were abused than females. Previous investigations have consistently shown that most elderly abused victims are female (Finklehor, 1983). The issue, then, becomes one of degree: Is abuse against men by women less serious? Of the 16 physically abused men in the 1988 study, only one said he suffered injury. Significantly, eight of the female victims suffered injury. A similar difference emerged on questions about emotional upset. When asked how upset they were by the violence, all but one of the women responded "very upset". In contrast, less than half of the abused men reported such a high level of emotional upset. The abused women thus suffered more physical and psychological consequences from the violence than the men.

ROLES, IDENTITY AND CRISIS

Identity is not immutable but subject to change over time, depending on the nature of the social situation and the "fit" of one's identity with the social context. Vital roles are symbols of identity, they are a basis of identification: "I am a wife". Helen Harris Perlman (1968) speaks of certain roles as "vital" because they are so interlaced with the personality, so deep driving in their significance to the person's feelings, perceptions, self-concept, and interpersonal relationships that they are essential to his or her total well-being. When a crisis occurs, the vital center is threatened and the individual attempts to cope. When this fails, the person experiences identity loss which may result in a crisis state. Crisis is frequently associated with loss.

Crises can result in ineffective psychosocial functioning. Certain life events precipitate crisis: death, job loss, marital separation. However, the events alone do not evoke crises. A person's perception, interpretation, and reaction to an event determine whether the person develops a crisis (Dixon and Sands, 1983). A crisis occurs when an event is perceived as a threat to a person's self-concept and the integration of self-validating role relationships. Under such circumstances, vital sources of affirmation of one's sense of personal identity are impaired. Because identity contributes to the wholeness or integrity of a person, such threats to integrity as illness are capable of causing disequilibrium.

In a longitudinal study by Klein, Dean and Bogdonoff (1967) of chronically ill patients and their spouses, support was found for the thesis that development of illness in the family is attended by role failure. This leads to interpersonal tension and psychological distress in both partners.

Because women generally marry older men and also live longer, they are much more likely to assume the caregiving role than the husband. In old age a man often seems to depend more on his wife than she on him.

LONELINESS

Like other psychological states, loneliness is difficult to define. It is characterized, in varying degrees, by marked feelings of loss, distress, separation, and isolation (Fromm-Reichmann, 1959; Townsend, 1957). Ordinary loneliness is caused either by emotional or social isolation and is associated with the commonplace feelings of boredom, emptiness, exclusion, and self- pity.

Any discussion of loneliness requires that attention be drawn to the aspects of gender differences. Past studies of gender differences in loneliness appear confusing. Russell, Peplau, and Cutrona (1980) claim that research has not indicated any gender difference in loneliness. On the contrary, Weiss (1973) presented survey evidence which showed that women were more apt to be lonely than men. Disparate conclusions appear to be related to measurement. Russell's study assessed loneliness among a sample of college students. Weiss based his approach on a direct inquiry of respondents who were asked to identify themselves as lonely or not.

That loneliness is reported to be more characteristic of women is explained by Borys and Perlman (1985):

1) If low self-esteem is associated with being lonely (Perlman and Peplau, 1981), and women are lower in self- esteem, then one would expect more women than men to be lonely;

2) Some scholars have argued that it is culturally more acceptable for women to express loneliness than men. Perhaps when faced with stress men are more likely to report somatic complaints, whereas women are likely to report affective distress (Hammen and Padesky, 1977). Other writers (Gove and Tudor, 1973) have argued that women's roles are simply more frustrating and less rewarding than men's;

3) Women consider interpersonal relationships more important than do men. Deficiencies in their social relationships may be more noteworthy and unpleasant for women;

4) Gender differences in loneliness might be explained in terms of genetic, hormonal or physiological factors;

Stokes and Levin (1986) suggested that women focus more on the qualities of dyadic relationships than men, who tend to be more group oriented in their friendships. Female college students reported themselves to be less lonely and to disclose more to their friends than did male subjects. According to their results, men and women may use different standards to evaluate loneliness. This finding underscores the importance of gender in research which examines loneliness, and results must be interpreted with these differences in mind.

Loneliness is often assumed to be a consequence of growing old. Of the total population 65 and older, 12% to 40% are identified as lonely (Creecy, Berg and Wright, 1985). Being alone is not necessarily associated with loneliness for some elderly people. Larson, Zuzanek and Mannell (1985) found that older adults neither need nor desire constant companionship. Among the married, many chose and cherished the opportunity to be alone. Among the unmarried, particularly those who lived alone, they appreciated being alone less. Marital status was the dependent variable in demonstrating the relationship between loneliness and the elderly. Results of a study of Swedish elderly (Berg et al., 1981) indicated that the loss of a spouse is the single most important factor contributing to loneliness.

Qualls, Norfleet and Harder (1986) studied loneliness in spousal caregivers of the physically and intellectually impaired aging. They suggested that losses in the marital relationship incurred as a function of impairment are not reported as producing loneliness or dissatisfaction with the marital relationship. Within the elderly group, loneliness has been associated with the incidence of endogenous depression and suicide (Breed, 1967; Payne, 1975).

DEPRESSION

It is important to distinguish loneliness from depression. Transitory loneliness, largely situational, comes and goes in the lives of all people. Those afflicted with chronic loneliness, however, tend to blame themselves for their condition and score higher on depression scales (Peplau, Russell and Helm, 1979). Depression, in these cases, appears more related to internal blame or cognitive factors than to external realities.

Richman and Flaherty (1985) studied beginning medical students to determine whether personality and social support are independent or highly correlated and how either of these variables protect against the development of depressive symptoms. Results indicated that internal-external locus of control and interpersonal dependency manifest a stronger relationship to depressive symptomatology than social supports. Interpersonal dependency was significantly correlated with social supports. Internal resources appeared to play a stronger role in protecting against the onset of depressive symptoms than did external resources. The person with a high level of interpersonal dependency appears to motivate the search for and satisfaction with external supports.

Depression in the Elderly

Mental health impairment is more frequently found among the elderly (Srole and Fischer, 1980). In a study by Blazer, Hughes and George (1987), the prevalence of significant depressive symptoms in a sample of over 1300 community elderly was 27%. Nearly 19% had dysphoric symptoms. Although less than 1% were experiencing major depression, they were likely to report negative life events and poor social relations. The most obvious explanation for increased depression among the elderly is that bereavement and decreased life satisfaction are more common in later life.

The prevalence and demography of depressive symptoms in the elderly was studied by Borson et al. (1986). In a large sample of elderly men seen in a primary care setting, 24% of the respondents reported clinically significant depressive symptoms. The prevalence of major depressive disorders was estimated at 10%. Marital separation or divorce and physical disability affecting employment were strongly associated with high depression scores, whereas the normal stresses of aging, such as widowhood, retirement, and social isolation were not. The association of marital loss with high depression scores is hardly surprising. Its specificity for separation and divorce, but not widowhood, however, is notable.

Bandura, a cognitive theorist, found one's concept of self-efficacy to be linked to the initiation and maintenance of coping behaviors (1982; Bandura, Adams and Beyer, 1977) Holohan and Holohan (1987) studied personal (self-efficacy) and environmental (social support) resources and their relationship to depression in a sample of 52 community elderly. Perceived self-efficacy relating to social support was assessed by asking respondents how they had handled several social concerns; for example, loneliness. Results indicated that ongoing depression may influence one's perception of self-efficacy and one's efforts to maintain behaviors that enable the older person to obtain a sufficient level of social support.

Spousal Depression

In a study by Mitchell, Cronkite and Moos (1983) normal couples and couples in which one partner was depressed were compared on life events, ongoing strains, coping responses, family support and depression. Depressed patients experienced more stress and possessed fewer of the personal and social resources that might moderate its impact. Spouses of depressed patients had higher levels of depression than control subjects. Negative life events, coping, and family support were directly related to depression. Research has shown that the pressures of dealing with an impaired family member can influence one's own psychological well-being (Finney et al., 1983). In a comparative study by Stommel, Given and Given. (1988), spouses who had institutionalized their husband or wife had higher levels of depression than those who cared for their spouse in the home. Findings support the view that caregiver depression is independent of the objective caregiver situation and that depression among caregivers should be treated like a personality variable. Stommel et al., conclude that psychological reaction variables which are used to measure burden among caregivers cannot be used to make policy. Additional services would not change the depressed caregiver's perception of burden.

Anticipatory Bereavement

Anticipatory grief refers to any grief occurring prior to an actual loss and is typically observed in situations where there is an awareness of the impending loss. Some authors have suggested that anticipatory grief may facilitate adjustment to bereavement because of the opportunity to engage in grieving prior to the death of the loved one (Arkin, 1974; Wiseman, 1974). By the time the actual loss occurs, the survivor supposedly has completed part of the mourning necessary for adapting to bereavement (Freud, 1917; Parkes, 1964).

Elderly persons are likely to anticipate the death of a spouse, as elderly individuals are most likely to experience chronic illnesses which culminate in death. Older women may be especially vigilant, because widowhood is a life event characteristic of this stage of the life cycle (Neugarten, 1977). As in chronic illness, nursing home placement can signal finality.

A study by Hill, Thompson and Gallagher, (1988) examined the role of anticipatory bereavement in the adjustment of older women to widowhood. Expectation of death was not related to better adjustment to bereavement in older women. Although this finding contradicts some of the theoretical and clinical speculations regarding anticipatory grief, the findings are consistent with several other studies.

Ball (1977) concluded that the lack of relationship between death expectancy and subsequent adjustment may be more characteristic of older adults than younger adults who, unlike their older counterparts, did show a better adjustment to bereavement when they anticipated, or were aware of, the impending death of their spouse. Yet results from Hill, Thompson and Gallagher (1988) indicated that engaging in spontaneous rehearsal was not related to better or poorer adjustment to bereavement. Those who engage in spontaneous rehearsal strategies may be less able to cope effectively to begin with, and only engage in rehearsal strategies in an unsuccessful effort to compensate for their inability to deal with the threat of widowhood. Had quality of rehearsal strategies been examined, the findings might have been different. The group who expected the death of their husband rated themselves in better mental health after their spouse's death than before. Widows who are expecting the death of their spouse may experience their greatest distress during the course of their husband's illness, and the death itself is a mixture of sorrow and relief. Following the death, they appeared no more or less distressed than widows who have lost their spouse unexpectedly.

Flaherty et al. (1987), found that the ability to adjust to widowhood was dependent on assessment of marital satisfaction. Those wives who characterized their marriages as happy were better adjusted following the death of their spouse than those who described their marriage as conflicted.

Studies of the effects of anticipatory bereavement on the adjustment to widowhood have been inconclusive. Separate studies in this area include assessment of the physical and emotional health of the widows and levels of marital satisfaction as indicators of adjustment. Future studies would do well to incorporate these three variables and to include an inventory of social supports as well as an assessment of the quality of the anticipatory bereavement behavior.

RETIREMENT

Although retirement is consistently characterized as a stressful life event, especially for men (Reichard, Livson and Peterson, 1962; Rollins and Feldman, 1970), evidence tends to be indirect and contradictory. Relatively little evidence documents how stressful retirees actually find their experience.

A study by Bosse, et al. (1988) of 676 male retirees and 840 male workers, using a list of 31 stressful life events, found that one's own retirement and the spouse's retirement were the two least stressful. Twice as many workers reported work problems as retirees reported retirement problems. The principal predictors of retirement stress were poor health and financial problems. The effect of the men's retirement on their wives was not examined.

Increased marital discord has been associated with retirement stress (Hill and Dorfman, 1982; Keating and Cole, 1980; Szinovacz, 1980). Others have found that retirement has little impact on marriage (Dressler, 1973).

SUMMARY

Older marriages are distinguishable by their commitment, stability and satisfaction. However, if a woman survives a long-term marriage, it may portend that her role as a wife will come to include that of caregiver to an ill and dependent husband. The satisfaction derived from a lifelong commitment to a spouse seems to provide the emotional foundation which helps her face crises. Despite this, external factors, such as nursing home placement of a spouse, may impinge on the older person's ability to engage social supports and avoid depression.

The women's movement of the '70's and the battered women's groups have given little attention to the elderly wife abused by an aging husband. Studies of younger abused women cannot automatically be extrapolated to an older group (Kosberg, 1988). The proliferation of elder abuse studies in the '80's focused on "granny bashing" and the problem of elderly abused by adult children. However, most elderly are cared for by their spouse.

Earlier studies of elder abuse were fraught with problems of definition which influence uniformity in methodology. A conference of 30 experts was unable to recommend a working definition of elder abuse (Family Research Laboratory, 1986). The assumption that elder abuse is relatively rare contributes to the conceptualization and methodological problems in the field. Most earlier studies failed to address issues of causation of elder abuse. The hypothesis that the dependency of the victim on the abuser is a primary cause of elder abuse is not supported.

THE RESEARCH PROBLEM

STATEMENT OF THE PROBLEM

This research was concerned with the effect of nursing home placement on the wives of residents. The impact of placement on the wives was assessed by several tested instruments and a guided interview designed for this study.

Do the changes encountered by placement of a husband place these wives at risk, and, if so, what interventions are appropriate?

METHODOLOGY AND DESIGN

An exploratory research design was used to describe the relationships between wives and their institutionalized husbands. The study was also descriptive in that the wives related in their own words their experiences and the effects of institutionalization on their marriage. The study used content analysis of qualitative data. Three survey instruments were added to corroborate responses to a guided interview.

SAMPLING PROCEDURE

At the study's inception it was hoped that the effects of institutionalization on men and women could be compared. Obtaining sufficient numbers of men for an adequate sample proved to be difficult, as the distribution of women to men in the nursing homes was approximately three to one.

Only one criterion of eligibility was used for the study: that the husband had resided in the nursing home at least three months prior to the interview. The choice of this time frame reflects a pivotal point in the course of nursing home experience. One third of those transferred to nursing homes stabilize within three months (Bartlett, 1989).

It was intended initially that the entire sample would be drawn from one institution, the largest nursing home in the State of Illinois. This home was the primary source of cases; however, to obtain an adequate sample, several other nursing homes were also included.

The primary source of the sample was a teaching nursing home in a near western suburb of Chicago that had a predominantly White ethnic population of residents of Eastern European descent. Of 450 residents at this home, 33 male residents had been living with their spouse at the time of placement, and had been placed for a period of three months or more. Letters were sent to each of the wives explaining the study and requesting participation (see Appendix A). The letter was endorsed by the nursing home and allowed potential participants an opportunity to consider the credibility of the study and the investigator. Follow-up calls were made a week later. Fourteen wives agreed to participate. In addition, five participants from a Jewish nursing home in a northern suburb were contacted initially by the administrator; all five agreed to take part in the study. Five participants from other homes were referred by professional contacts and were included in the sample, making the total number of participants 24.

Those wives who declined to be interviewed stated that they were too ill themselves to participate, were "not interested", or that the husband had died or deteriorated. A few wives spent quite a bit of time in telephone conversations with the researcher convinced they "would have nothing to say", but these conversations alluded to coping styles and support systems.

LIMITATIONS OF THE SAMPLE

1) This study involved a self-selected sample of 24 wives of nursing home residents. Husbands were not interviewed due primarily to the extent of their cognitive impairments.
2) With a small sample, attempts to generalize to a larger population are speculative at best.
3) There was no direct way of verifying if the wives' testimony in regard to abuse was indeed factual. However, their version of reality was accepted by the interviewer.

DATA COLLECTION

The guided interview is a desirable technique for studying the process of relationships, and content analysis is a suitable method for understanding qualitative data. All interviews were conducted by the researcher and all participants signed consent forms (see Appendix B). Every subject was given a code number to protect anonymity and confidentiality.

Subjects were assured anonymity of all taped and written materials. Prior to and during each interview, the wives were encouraged to ask any questions they had concerning the study. Each subject was assigned a code number known only to the researcher. Prior to the interviews, approval for the research was obtained through the Institutional Review Board of the University of Illinois Hospital and through the nursing home's administrative review committee.

All interviews except one were audiotaped. One wife requested not to be taped. Her responses were written by hand by the interviewer.

Interviews ranged from one to two hours and averaged one hour. Interviews were scheduled at the wives' convenience. Field notes of the researcher's impressions of the interviews were made immediately following each session.

TOOLS AND TECHNIQUES

Three survey instruments were also administered: the Locke and Wallace Marital-Adjustment Scale (1959), the CES-D (Radloff, 1977), and the Hinton Scale (1981) (see Appendices D, E, and F). All three were chosen for their conceptual clarity and brevity.

The Marital Adjustment Scale

The first attempt to measure marital success by a numerical score was made by Hamilton (1929), involving thirteen items. More recent tests of marital adjustment have used a very large number of items (Burgess and Cottrell, 1939; Snyder, 1979; Terman and Oden, 1947). The length of these tests is their main disadvantage.

The Locke and Wallace Marital-Adjustment Scale (1959) used in this study was constructed from the most significant items taken from prior studies using the scale. In the standardization of the Locke and Wallace scale, a group of forty-eight persons known to be maladjusted in their marriage was matched for age and sex with forty-eight persons judged to be exceptionally well-adjusted. The assessment of "adjusted" or "maladjusted" was made experientially by friends who knew them well and by the referring agency. Respondents were predominantly young, white, educated, white-collar and professional, Protestant and urban. Items on the test included, for example, the extent of agreement or disagreement between spouses on sexual relations and philosophy of life. This test clearly differentiates quality of marital interaction. Since 1959 the Locke and Wallace Scale has been used widely, including application to an older population (Flaherty et al., 1987).

Possible scores on the Locke and Wallace Scale range from 2-158. Mean adjustment scores for the well-adjusted group were 135.9, whereas the mean score for the maladjusted group was only 71.7. Only seventeen percent of the maladjusted group achieved adjustment scores of one hundred or higher, whereas 96% of the well-adjusted group achieved scores of one hundred or more.

The CES-D, Center for Epidemiologic Studies, Depression Scale

A self-report depression scale, the CES-D (Radloff, 1977; see appendix E) is designed to measure depressive symptoms in the general population. The twenty items are symptoms associated with depression used in longer, previously validated scales. They include such items as "I felt lonely" , and "I felt sad", in reference to the past week. This scale, tested in household interview surveys and psychiatric settings, was found to have high internal consistency and adequate test-retest reliability. Validity was established by patterns of correlations with other self-report measures, by correlations with clinical ratings of depression, and by relationships with other variables which support its construct validity. The bias of social desirability was small. The relationships of the CES-D scores to life events are considered validation of its sensitivity to current mood state (Radloff, 1977).

Among the elderly, CES-D scores average between seven and nine. Stommel, Given and Given, (1988), in a longitudinal study of 181 caregivers, found an average CES-D score of 14, with a range of depressive scores between 0 and 41. Forty percent of the sample were found to be clinically depressed. The instrument was administered at intake, 6 months and 12 months later, and demonstrated stable results over time.

The Hinton Scale

The interview included the Hinton Scale (1981), a series of five pairs of circles designed to measure affective and emotional proximity. Subjects were asked to choose the pair of circles which best represent their feelings of closeness to their spouse, before the husband's illness and after he was placed in the nursing home.

Health and Demographics

The health of the participant and her spouse were assessed by a short inventory developed for this study (see Appendix G). Personal background and demographic information on the couple was gathered to determine the socioeconomic background of the sample (see Appendix H).

INTERVIEW PROCESS

A guided interview was designed (see Appendix C) to focus on characteristics of the marriage before the illness of the husband, while the wife was a caregiver at home, her present feelings, and her perceptions of the future.

Lofland (1971) described the interview process as a "guided conversation".

Its object is not to elicit choices between alternative answers to pre-formed questions but, rather, to elicit from the interviewee what is considered important relative to a given topic, the description of some situation being explored. Its object is to carry on a guided conversation and to elicit rich, detailed materials that can be used in qualitative analysis. Its object is to find out what kinds of things are happening, rather than to determine the frequency of predetermined kinds of things that the researcher already believes can happen. (p. 76)

The wives were encouraged to share their experiences as they perceived them. Insights were gained from the wives' definitions and descriptions of their situations which, in turn, gave meaning to their relationships. This interactional approach compels the investigator to understand the relationship from the subject's perspective. Interest in the dynamics of the institutionalized marriage provided the direction and impetus for inquiry.

CODING OF RESPONSES

The first five audiotapes were transcribed by the author and immediately coded. Two research assistants independently transcribed the remaining taped interviews.

Each interview was coded before the next interview was conducted. After the transcripts were coded they were copied and a set filed in a separate location in order to protect the data, in case the set was lost. Before each transcript was cut and affixed to index cards, the data from the instrument package were transferred to a summary grid table in order to examine the data.

The content of the audiotaped interviews was analyzed by adapting six major categories from a coding scheme developed by Bogdan and Biklen (1982). Their original scheme provided eight categories:
(1) setting/context: general information on surroundings;
(2) definition of the situation: how people define the setting;
(3) perspectives: ways of thinking, orientation;
(4) ways of thinking about people and objects: more detailed than the above;
(5) process: sequences, flow, changes over time;
(6) activities: regularly occurring kinds of behavior;
(7) events: specific activities;
(8) strategies: ways of accomplishing things.

For this study, "ways of thinking about people and objects" was renamed "relationships".
Due to lack of responses, two categories, "setting/context" and "activities", were eliminated. The six major categories of the coding scheme are defined and illustrated from the subjects' responses:

(1)   DEFINITION   OF   THE   SITUATION: combination   of circumstances at a given time -- factual background, history -- concrete and factual description of the nursing home, husband's illness, caregiving, wives' reality.
>   Example:
>   "I would give him therapy every day and it would be noon by the time I would be through with him. Sometimes he would he very irritable and I can understand this because even though his left side is paralyzed, he still has pain and any movement hurts him and he could strike out at me and really say nasty things to me and I would sometimes say nasty things to him."

(2) PERSPECTIVES: perceptions, points of view, ways of thinking, feelings, hopes, dreams, needs, wishes, issues, considerations, opinions -- the meaning of a situation.
>   Example:
>   "It was a good marriage. We had our ups and downs, but we had an unusually good marriage. You know, we met

and we fell in love and that was it. There were just never
any doubts."

(3) PROCESSES: series of events over time, changes by which
something develops a particular method of doing something which
involves several steps.

> Example:
> "Well, for so many years I wasn't able to get to church
> with Dad and I just fell away. I still go, don't get me
> wrong, but I am not active like I was."

(4) STRATEGIES: a plan or action with a purpose, problem solving,
coping techniques, solutions.

> Example:
> "I went for help myself to the Family Service. I went to
> the sessions and it helped a lot. We have that in our area
> and that's how I got help for my husband, through them.
> And I've tried everything I could. Then I had them come
> to the house. I don't know if that has a bearing on it.
> They came a few times."

(5) EVENTS: an important occurrence, a result, an outcome, a
specific activity.

> Example:
> "When he retired he had a bad time."

(6) RELATIONSHIPS: reference to relevant personal connections, a
state of relatedness.

> Example:
> "If I complain too much my daughter-in-law tells me off.
> I guess she doesn't think my attitude is right."

The dominant theme of each response was coded. "Conceptual
memos" and ideas were noted in the margins of the coding cards. For
example, "I've had to learn to do a lot of things I never knew how to
do before", had the notation "adaptability" in the margin. The
transcribed copy was then cut and arranged by codes, and affixed to a
corresponding color-coded 5" x 8" index card for easy retrieval.

To classify the collection of information, a filing system was developed and arranged by topics in designated folders. A log contained daily entries on the time spent on the project and included reading time, interviews, discussions with others, travel time, data collection, analysis and writing.

THE INTERVIEW

Content analysis of the semi-structured interview was used to discover how wives characterize their relationships with their institutionalized husbands. The process of inquiry became the focus of analysis, rather than the respondents themselves. This method of inquiry supported the pursuit of meanings and interpretations identified by the wives.

RELIABILITY AND VALIDITY

Much of the interview process relied on retrospection by the wives. Recall of past perceptions of the marital relationship raises issues of the reliability and validity of qualitative data. How does one make sense of another's social world?

Wiseman (1974) addresses the issues and reliability of qualitative data. In judging the validity and usefulness of data, she suggested the following rules:

1. Assume that no one is lying.
2. If you must choose between an official's story and that of an individual (that is, institution versus individual) -- most likely the institution is not being totally honest.
3. There is nothing that happens or that people tell you about that "doesn't make any sense". It is part of their lives. They think it makes sense.
4. Assume that human beings may not be very smart in the decisions they make, but they do the very best they can.
5. There is usually nothing that people tell you or that you will see that is truly irrelevant to your study.
6. There is no such thing as absolute truth. All the most objective researcher can report is his version of the actions and decisions of others and how they see the world. (pp. 325-326.)

One must remember that interviews reveal the subjects' view of their world. The data become reliable and significant when they reveal consistent findings about the nature of the problems for the spouse involved in institutionalization. This occurred in regard to the findings of abuse, role ambivalence and financial hardship.

Miles and Huberman (1984) indicate that the use of more than one method of inquiry, triangulation, addresses issues of reliability. This study incorporated a guided interview, three survey instruments and field notes. Inter-rater reliability of approximately 80% was achieved using two independent raters who coded the same interview. A high rate of internal consistency was reached by coding each interview immediately and recoding the same interview again a few days later. A daily log was kept in which all changes and the reasons were recorded.

SUMMARY

Few data are available on the impact of nursing home care from the perspective of the spouse in the community. Hence, the goal of this research was to discover meanings and concerns articulated by those living through the experience. A qualitative research design was used to answer the question, "What is the impact of the husband's placement on their wives?"

FINDINGS FROM THE INSTRUMENTS

THE LOCKE AND WALLACE (1959) MARITAL ADJUSTMENT SCALE

The wives' scores on the Marital Adjustment Scale ranged from 42 - 139, with a mean of 116.2 (see Table I, on the following page). This placed them between the well-adjusted mean of 135.9 and the maladjusted mean of 71.7.

Fourteen of the 22 respondents scored between 120 - 139, which is a range between the group mean and the highest score and includes the well-adjusted mean score of 135.9. These findings coincide with the results of the Hinton Scale, which indicated in a visual analog that half of the sample (11) perceived a high degree of marital closeness, both before the husband's illness and after placement. The woman who scored the lowest score (72) had lived with an alcoholic husband who had abused her verbally and physically throughout the 55 years of marriage.

THE HINTON SCALE

On the Hinton Scale (1981), described previously on page 23 and included as Appendix F, a total of 16 of 22 wives indicated the greatest degree of closeness prior to their husband's illness by choosing set A of the circles. Five wives chose the second set of circles, B. Only one chose set C as an indicator of marital closeness prior to the husband's illness.

---

1 For the Marital Adjutment and Hinton Scales, the findings are based on a sample of 22, as two sets of data were unusable due to lack of response. The CES-D findings are based on a sample of 23.

Table 1
The Locke and Wallace Marital Adjustment Scale

Subjects

Item	001	002	003	004	005	006	007	008	009	010	011	012	013	014	015	016	017	018	119	020	021	022	023	024
1. Happiness	35	15	35	15	15	15	35	25		20	15	35	30	35	35	15	35		30	30	25	30	35	15
2. Finances	1	2	1	2	1	1	1	2		2	2	1	1	2	1	1	2		1	1	1	1	1	1
3. Recreation	2	1	1	2	1	1	1	2		1	2	2	1	2	2	1	1		1	1	2	2	2	4
4. Affection	1	1	2	1	1	1	1	1		1	1	1	1	1	1	1	1		2	1	2	1	1	1
5. Friends	1	1	1	1	1	2	1	2		1	2	1	2	2	1	3	1		2	2	1	1	1	2
6. Sex	2	2	2	1	1	2	2	2		2	2	1	2	1	1		1		3	1	2			
7. Convention	2	2	1	1	1	2	3			2	1	1	1	2	1	2	1		1	1	1	1	3	3
8. Philosophy	1	3	1	2	3	2		3		1	1		1	1	2	1	2		2	2	2	1	1	1
9. In-Laws	1			1	1		1	1		4	3	1	1	1		1			2	1	1	2		
10. Disagree	3	3	3	3	1	3	1	3		3	2	3	3	3	3	3	3		2	2	3	3		
11. Out interests	1	2	2	2	2	3	2	2		2	2	3	1	1	2	3	2		2	2	1	2	2	2
12. Leisure	1	3	1	2	2	2	2	1		3	3	1	2	2	3	1			2	3	1	1	3	3
13. Wish not wed	3	2	3	3	2	4	4	4		3	2	3	4	4	4	4	4		3	4	4	4	4	4
14. Marry same	1	1	1	1	1	1	1	1		1	3	1	1	1	1	1	1		1	1	1	1	1	
15. Confide	4	3	2	3	2	3	3	3		4	3	4	3	3	3	4	4		3	4	2	3	1	4
Weighted Score	138	98	127	115	86	101	123	128	0	110	77	128	131	136	131	116	139	0	106	120	123	131	121	72

Possible Range of Scores 2 - 158
Well Adjusted Mean 135.9
Maladjusted Mean 71.7
6 incomplete data (responses to individual questions missing)

Actual Results   N = 22
Mean   116.2
Range   42 - 139

Five other wives felt furthest from their husbands after placement as reflected by their choice of set of the circles. Three of these five had felt closest (A) to their spouse prior to the onset of illness.

Despite the marital disruption, changes in residence, and reference to "married widowhood", half of the wives (11 of the 22 who completed the instrument) felt as close to their husbands in the nursing home as they did prior to their husband's illness.

The three wives who felt their relationship had gone from closest to furthest (A to E) had encountered specific insults:

One wife was advocating for DNR (do not resuscitate) status for her husband, who had been bedridden for years, was incontinent, contracted and did not speak. Her husband had Alzheimer's and was being fed through a tube. This wife was quite irate that her husband's Living Will was not honored and felt that it would be merciful to let him die in the event that he suffered a cardiac arrest.

Another wife was angry at a system which would allow her husband, a stroke victim, to be transferred from one home to another when his veteran's benefits were terminated. This man was occasionally alert and communicative.

A woman who had been abused by an alcoholic husband with Alzheimer's for 17 years felt relief and distance as a result of placement. She had felt close to her husband because they had seven children together, and because she had cared for him for so many years at home.

Three of the four wives whose levels of marital closeness dropped three sets of circles post-placement (2 from B to E, 2 from A to D) were also found to be depressed according to their CES-D scores. It is possible that the wives in this sample changed their views about their marriage over time, and that the high level of marital satisfaction attributed to the relationship prior to the husband's illness was not a stable variable throughout the lifetime of the marriage, and was negatively affected by the husband's illness and placement. However, all of the wives said they had never wished they had not married and they would probably marry the same person again, when questioned in the Marital Assessment Scale.

THE CES-D SCALE

Sixty percent, or fourteen of twenty-three wives, scored over sixteen (which is the cutoff score) on the CES- D Scale (Radloff, 1977), indicating depression. Scores ranged from 3 - 41. The average score was 19.

Length of time spent in the caregiving role does not appear to affect the incidence of depression. Caregivers may enter the caregiving situation with different levels of depression or dispositions toward depression. Most important, then, is the personal and psychological history of the caregiver.

In summary, the sample of wives in the study presented here reported high levels of marital satisfaction prior to their husband's illness; this finding may be influenced by the satisfaction derived from caregiving. This is consistent with older couples' reports of higher marital quality, as cited earlier (Anderson, Russell and Schumm, 1983).

FINDINGS FROM THE INTERVIEWS

RETIREMENT

Twenty wives in this study had worked full-time and for them, retirement was well-accepted. Four wives were still employed, at least part-time. Those who were housewives still considered themselves in that role. The effects of their husband's retirement on the spouse was often related in time to the onset of illness. Husbands were forced to retire from their jobs due to the manifestations of disease or illness. Consistent with Bosse's (1988) study, illness was a principal predictor of retirement stress for these couples.

Twelve husbands in the present study were "terminated" from their job, or forced to retire early because of their symptoms, such as confusion, aggressiveness and wandering. One husband was "phased out" of employment prior to retirement due to cutbacks in the industrial sector of the economy. As one wife stated,

Part of it [the Alzheimer's] was triggered by the fact that after 40 years they were kind of laying him off and...well, they terminated...his laying off to him was the same as being fired. 'Cause they wanted all young guys. They didn't want none of the old guys. They done it to all of the guys. It was like five of them that were there for years, they were getting four weeks paid vacation and so they didn't want that. They [the employer] wanted to get all the new guys they could start with cheaper wages.

The wives described their husbands as diligent and responsible workers, committed to their employers. One example,

He was never late a day in his life. He didn't start 'til six but he'd leave home at four in the morning. Never took a day off. Except one day he had to take off, we had to go downtown on business, and they thought he died. They wouldn't believe that he... so they sent guys over to check on him. That's how much time he took off.

33

One wife described the behavior which forced her husband to retire. His wandering episodes were often attempts to "get to work",

I had to sleep with one eye open because I was always afraid he was going to leave, because he would get up during the night and he didn't know what time it was. Sometimes he didn't know if it would start getting dark. He didn't know if it was evening or if it was morning. You know, I just never knew when he was going to disappear.

One husband, who suffered from depression, was depicted by his wife, "When he retired he had a bad time". Her husband subsequently slid into a major depression.

He worked for Sears, and he was in stocks, bonds. He worked physically hard. He worked. He walked a lot. Worked in the mail order. He was a good worker, never took days off.

Employment and the workplace are often important sources of identity and meaning. In most of these cases, the husband's condition forced his retirement. Blau (1973) suggested retirement is stressful as it constitutes a "role exit" without entry into a new role. For almost half of the husbands in this study, retirement signalled an exit from the role as breadwinner and entrance into the role of dependent patient. Wives assumed new roles as caregivers.

FACING THE ILLNESS

Longitudinal analysis of subjective feelings of burden among elderly spouses suggests that caregivers' ability to tolerate problem behavior actually increases even as the disease progresses (Zarit, S., Todd, P. and Zarit, J., 1986). However, as their husbands became ill and increasingly dependent, the wives experienced disruptive changes. These shifts were described by the wives in various ways.

One wife described her husband's debilitating depression,

He just gave up. He gave up living...Depression is a terrible disease, did you know that? Terrible, you just give up. You just don't care about anything. You don't live. You don't plan nothing.

One wife commented on the shock of facing a chronic illness when her husband suffered his first stroke,

It's sort of devastating to have your whole life changed. In all our wildest dreams, we'd never imagined anyone being sick, and either one of us ending up this way. We just didn't plan on it. Sort of stupid.

A morbid scenario was depicted by a wife who had her own medical problems. When her husband was at home she struggled daily to take him outdoors. He was a stroke victim and almost dead weight,

I told him, "One of these days I'm going to be laying on top of you and I'm going to be dead, and then what's going to happen? Our son comes here someday," I said, "and he'll put us both in the bag and we'll be buried." I told him, "I wish you could help me more," but you know, he was getting too weak.

THE DECISION TO PLACE

In most cases, a significant event occurred to make nursing home placement the only feasible alternative. Five wives had experienced their own illnesses or accidents which necessitated the placement of their husbands. One such crisis is explained by a wife who had tried to use the "rest home" for respite care,

Oh, it had to be. It happened when my daughter was at home and a friend was there when this happened. But I felt the seizure coming on and, when I had these seizures I go completely out, I don't remember anything about them. And when I came to I was in the hospital, and they called the rescue squad to take me in. Well, what was M. going to do? All she could do was call the rest home and have them bring their van over and take him back to the rest home. Well, then I was in the hospital for over a week. And so when I came home, I knew I could never take care of him at home again. It isn't fair to my family, it isn't fair to me, well, I just couldn't do it. And that was the reason for the decision to take him over there. There was just no other way.

A vivid account by one wife, whose husband had Alzheimer's disease, illustrates the basis for placement,

Three times he tried to strangle me, and then from the back. He was just going behind me in the kitchen but I had a funny feeling, because he passed like a cat, and suddenly I felt that he grabbed me by the neck. But I jumped and I just pushed him away and I ran downstairs to my landlady and I told her I didn't know what to do. And when he came back he didn't know it. The next morning he felt bad. But I still didn't know what it is, what is happening, until my son came from Boston and he took him to the hospital. And they made different tests. He was seven or eight days in the psychiatric unit of the hospital. The doctor, he told me it is Alzheimer's disease.

When asked if her husband had ever been violent or threatening, one wife responded,

Once he did. I went to change him and he was so angry, he said to me, "I'll kill you." He was already pretty well in Alzheimer's then. So the doctor said, "You better do something with him, because he's going to hurt you. 'Cause I know how violent he'll get. We're trying to examine him and it took three doctors to hold him still. He was real nasty." So I thought, well, maybe they are right.

For one wife, an incident of wandering by her husband alerted the rest of the family to the severity of the situation. It was the evidence the wife needed to convince other family members that her husband could not continue to live at home. Their son denied his father's illness until this incident. He did not visit his father in the nursing home.

Wives spoke of their feelings about institutionalizing their husbands. One woman became acutely aware of the need for restraint,

You know there comes a time when your patience runs out. Before I would start being mean to him, or abuse him, I felt I better not. I can't be mean to him. I have to put him in a home.

The most profound loss these women experienced was the loss of the marital relationship, which was manifested by the lack of communication and intimacy. One woman described what was missing from her relationship with her husband,

> I don't have his arm around me at night. He's been grabbing me and hugging me lately and kissing me, which he hasn't done for a long time. And one day he told me he loved me. That made me feel good....

This wife was a daily visitor to her husband in the nursing home.

In contrast, the previous interview had been with a woman who was described by her son as unable to get in touch with her feelings ... "she hasn't cried yet." Initially this wife appeared quite controlled, very pleasant and interested in satisfying the interviewer. Towards the end of the interview, when I asked her what had been most difficult about the placement, she broke down. She recalled the time she had to ask her husband to sign the papers to transfer the family farm to her: "He asked me, 'Don't you love me?'" At this point she also revealed that her son had said she "needed to cry." This wife mailed me a note later to say that she was glad to have had the opportunity to help me with my study. Perhaps she was also glad to have had what must have been a cathartic experience. At painful points in the interview, with two exceptions, all wives shed some tears.

Retirement, illness, and institutionalization were all significant transitions in the lives of these couples. As the husband's illness progressed, wives became increasingly aware of the limitations of home care, but did not feel a nursing home to be an acceptable option. At the point of the institutionalization, these women had come to realize that they could no longer jeopardize their own health and well-being. Several wives had had medical crises of their own, and a few were aware of the physical threat of violence by husbands who were victims of disease. A crisis most often precipitated nursing home placement.

The husbands in this study, while they were still at home, had been quite needy and demanding, often requiring 24-hour care. Confusion, incontinence, wandering, combative behavior, and the inability to communicate were characteristics of illnesses dealt with by these wives. The wives adapted and accepted their role over the caregiving years. "There was no choice, you just did it," one wife said.

The powerful commitment and strength of these wives to continue caregiving at home was based on happy marriages prior to their husband's illness. Commitment may provide the security in the relationship that makes it possible for these wives to take the risk and actively grapple with problems. The meaning of marriage to these women was demonstrated by strong devotion and loyalty in an adverse situation. Several of the wives believed that they would be taken care of reciprocally by their husbands, had the situation been reversed.

Once the husband had been transferred to a nursing home, the separation process had begun, emotionally and physically. The wives experienced the conflicting emotions of relief that their husband was institutionalized, yet most wished they were still able to care for their husbands at home. Institutionalization challenged the wives' roles as caregivers as the situation required a change in established behaviors, role patterns, self-concept, and attitudes.

Most of the wives had no prior experience with nursing homes and rarely, if ever, entertained placement as an option while serving as long-term caregivers in their own homes. Most of the women did not anticipate such a course of events as chronic illness, caregiving, and eventual placement of their husbands in a nursing home. For half of the wives, placement activated anticipatory bereavement strategies, such as preparations for funerals, pursuit of living wills, liquidation of their husbands' assets and discussions of feelings regarding the eventual death of their husbands.

FREQUENCY OF VISITS

Ten of the wives visited their husbands daily. One woman visited her husband daily from 11 am until 8 pm. Two came twice a month, one because she was dependent on her housekeeper for transportation, and another because she lived quite a distance. At 87 she still drove and planned her visits for alternate Sunday mornings. She was on the road at 7 am in order to avoid heavy traffic while she drove for an hour to reach the nursing home. The rest of the wives visited three to four times a week. Almost all lived within five miles of the nursing home.

The high frequency of visits by the wives was independent of the husband's ability to communicate. One wife had cared for her husband at home for eleven years before he was placed in a nursing home six months prior. A victim of several strokes and Parkinson's disease, her husband was unable to converse: "I can't communicate with him.

Sometimes I just sit there, maybe for two hours, and he's just out of it completely." She also lamented the lack of privacy in the nursing home: "I feel bad that there's no place you can go with your husband and just sit with him, just to be alone."

ROLE TRANSITIONS / PROCESSES

The wives in this study underwent two distinct transitions in later marrie.l life. The first occurred when their husbands became ill. One third of the wives related their husband's retirement to his illness. Developing symptoms or an acute event forced the men to leave their jobs, or else the illness began soon after the husband retired. This began the wives' careers as in-home caregivers. The second transition was the transfer of care of the husband to the institution.

At the time of the onset of illness, the husband's dependence was the issue. In the second transition, on which this study focuses, the issue was separation. Prior patterns of behavior, in each case, required adjustment. For wives to successfully adapt, they had to accept changes in routine, in identification of roles and tasks, and in their sense of self as wives and also as caregivers.

Illness and subsequent nursing home placement of a spouse are stressful events, as well as ongoing strains. This study found that nursing home placement of husbands forced the reassessment of caregiving roles and spousal identities for the wives which resulted in feelings of ambiguity. For a few, however, the outlook for a successful resolution to the ambiguity of nursing home placement was the merciful death of the husband.

Separation

Unfortunately, for some of the wives of this study, the family had been reduced to a unilateral relationship with a husband who was emotionally unavailable for support. While challenged by the adversity of their husband's illness and placement, they consistently demonstrated self-reliance. There were few reliable resources in cases where the couple had no children, when the wives were abandoned by family due to misunderstanding, or when restrictions on the wives' time prevented them from pursuing family or friends. They remained committed to their husbands and clung to the memories of a happy marriage.

The husband's transfer to a nursing home represented the beginning of a separation process and signalled an adjustment in the wives' perception of themselves and their marriage. This movement of the husband from home to nursing home created ambiguity for the wives which was reflected in statements about themselves and their relationships.

A wife reminisced about her hopes that her husband would improve from a depressive illness,

> I waited. Maybe he'd get better. But he didn't, so I waited about two years and I sold our motor home. We didn't go anywhere at all. Just wouldn't go anyplace. By 1981, we never went out. He just stayed in, didn't want anybody over to the house. I've been a grass widow since then.

After six years of caring for her husband at home, another woman was encouraged by her daughter to seek placement. Her husband's Alzheimer's disease had become worse and she was victimized by his violent outbursts, "He doesn't even know me anymore. It's just like I'm single. Like I've never even been married to him. He's not the same anymore."

One wife struggled with the nursing home to obtain "Do Not Resuscitate" status for her husband with Alzheimer's disease who was contracted, non-communicative, and had a feeding tube,

> I consider myself married, but I consider I don't have a husband. I don't know how to else to state it. I don't. I have no one that I can talk to. No one to take a walk with, no one to feed at home, to make a meal for. How else can I say it?

The loss of a sense of self was vividly expressed as she continued,

> I don't feel like a wife. I am just me now. I'm just nobody. That's just the way I feel. You can't have somebody for all those years and then you don't have nothin'.

For many, the self has meaning only in relationship to others. The human drama of empty and broken relationships brought about by illness and placement was poignantly portrayed by this group of wives.

Orientation: Present vs. Future

In addition to such changes in self-concept, other changes in attitude were evident, such as time orientation. Several wives were clearly oriented to the present and made statements such as, "I take one day at a time," or "I don't think about the future." Other wives verbalized wishes, fears and concrete plans for the future. Seven wives clearly stated they took "each day at a time," in response to probes about their plans for the future. In apparent efforts to cope, five wives said they never think about the future. One of the youngest wives, when asked about the future, said she felt "resentful." Neither she nor her husband had ever expected what had happened.

A very adamant wife, whose husband was in a vegetative state, had similar arrangements for herself and her husband:

I will not have a funeral any more. We're both going to be cremated. Nobody comes to see him. They don't want to see him like this, they don't want to see him dead. So I had all the arrangements made. The minute he dies he will be cremated. And the minute I die I go to be cremated, because I would never do to him what I wouldn't do to myself. And that's the way we're going. I have lots all paid for, cemetery all paid for, but it's not going to be used. Maybe someday I'll have them put the ashes there, that would be it. You get to feel like that.

Several wives revealed that they prayed for their husbands to die. One wife prayed that "the Lord would take me and my husband soon," so they would not be a burden on their children. With his death, they would both be relieved of pain and suffering. Other wives tried to plan in the event that their death preceded that of their husband's. Three wives mentioned that both they and their husbands had Living Wills but expressed concerns that they may not be honored in the nursing home. One woman was pursuing implementation of DNR (Do Not Resuscitate) orders for her husband in the nursing home. While one wife had negotiated the sale of the family farm, another contemplated selling her home. Another wife spoke of having obtained legal assistance to split the assets that she and her husband had jointly owned.

Hill, Thompson, and Gallagher (1988) described certain spontaneous rehearsal strategies used by widows prior to their husband's death, such as discussion of funeral arrangements, financial security, feelings about being left behind, and what the future would be like if the spouse died before them. Many of the wives in the present study actively prepared for their husband's further debilitation and eventual death, as well as their own. The language used by these wives to describe their marriage and themselves reflects the definite shift in situation, behavior, attitude, and orientation toward the future. Institutional marriage was portrayed as "married widowhood."

The Caregiver Role

Due to the husbands' cognitive and physical losses, the husbands were less active participants in the process of role redefinition. Once transfer of the husband to the nursing home occurred, the wife's role became one of monitoring the care he received. Fourteen wives felt like helpers to their husbands. These women voiced more control over their role within the nursing home. One wife said, for example, "I'm the boss." These women also felt more confident about the support they provided their husbands in the nursing home; they had that special emotional bond of marriage and time which could not be matched by any of the nursing home staff. By contrast, eight wives related that they felt less like their husband's primary caregiver and more like a visitor in the nursing home. One wife described this as being "on the sidelines."

Married Widows - Role Ambivalence

There is an old adage, "Love cannot last, but marriage must." The meaning of marriage for these wives was epitomized by the woman who said, "Marriage means caring for someone other than yourself." Perlman (1968) theorized that women obtain self-realization through marriage more often than men.

A marriage that is sustained through old age is enhanced by knowledge of the spouse which is accumulated over the years, along with a lifetime of rationalizations about the spouse's behavior. Habits, idiosyncracies, likes, and dislikes become well-known to each other. The wives spoke of how they felt they had special knowledge of their husband and his illness, which was not always well-received by the nursing home staff. Since the wives no longer cared for their husbands at home, they had lost a sense of control over their environment, as well as their relationship.

These wives felt there were no options other than caring in a special way for their husbands in the nursing home. Their role as wives was to provide the extra emotional and tactile stimulation through meaningful touch, which could not be expected from the nursing home staff. "There is always the lightning bond of communion (between loved ones) that touch and presence alone provides" (Perlman, 1968).

In some cases, the wives had not only lost the reciprocity of the husband/wife relationship, but were also abandoned by their children (most often sons), who did not understand the mother's continued attachment to her husband. Although they felt indispensable in some ways in the loving care they provided their husbands in the nursing home, the wives were uncertain of their role as defined by the institution. The lack of reciprocity within the marriage, coupled with the separateness imposed by placement, created a sense of limbo in regard to their self-definition. At least widowhood confirmed an undeniable role.

MAJOR CONCERNS

Finances

The wives lived on annual incomes which averaged $12,000. Yearly incomes ranged from "below" $5,000 to "more than" $20,000 (see Appendix H). Although most stated they were "getting along," they expressed much anxiety and uncertainty about their financial future. They just did not know what expenses lay ahead.

Seven wives stated their most immediate need was financial. They were insecure about the future. How would they maintain their household and continue to pay the price of nursing home placement? One wife's income was reduced from $1,300 a month to $300,

> You're supposed to pay your gas, lights and phone and house insurance and medical insurance, and I don't know how they expect you to do it.

When asked what would be of most help to her now, she replied, "To have all my bills paid up." Not only was the cost of nursing home care astronomical (approximately $2,000 per month), but certain therapies and medications were charged to the patient and billed to the wife.

Some had seen their savings depleted; others were in the process of watching their savings evaporate. One wife who felt strongly that her husband should be allowed to die was struggling, both emotionally and financially:

It takes every penny of his money, plus! And he gets a good pension both from Social Security and the union where he worked. It just covers the rooms.

She had transferred her husband from one nursing home to another for reasons of cost. "I just couldn't afford it. It was over $3,000 a month. I couldn't. The money would have all been gone."

Two wives whose assets were greater than the average retained legal counsel. In one case, the wife sought authority to liquidate property; in another, to cash in stocks and bonds.

Entitlement concerns were voiced by many of the wives. One salient issue was that of the husband's Social Security benefits. In most cases, the husband's Social Security check went directly to the nursing home and was considered lost income by the wives. Several wives were waiting approval of Medicaid benefits to cover the cost of their husband's care. Their savings had been exhausted. One wife complained about the cut in veteran's benefits. As a result, her husband would have to be transferred to another nursing home that would accept the reduced level of payment.

All of these women had participated at some time in the labor force. Most had worked in the service sector or held clerical positions. They did not understand how they could be in positions of financial dependence when they had worked and saved as couples most of their lives. It was a bitter irony. One wife railed against "an unjust system",

I know so many people that just live and travel and live and travel, "The State will pay for me." I never had that feeling. I saved. Where is it all going? Now I cannot use one penny of my husband's pension, not one penny of his money. Now if I hadn't worked I would have had to turn him over to the State. I would have had to. 'Cause what would I have to live on? Now I've got my $600 and I can draw out of my pension if I want. 'Cause I had that put in my own name right away, because I know my husband was sick then already. And there's nothing wrong in that. I worked 35 years for it. And I worked hard.

Financial uncertainty plagued the wives in this sample. Entitlements were an issue, which included the cutbacks in government programs. The overall cost of nursing home care was a source of dread and anxiety. These wives were saddled with concerns about their husband's care and condition, the cost of that care, and the burden of unfamiliar and inescapable responsibilities.

New Responsibilities

Baum and Baum (1980) contrasted the view of aging as a restrictive process with the view of old age as an opportunity for new experiences. It may be both restrictive and a source of new experiences. The meaning of "new" experiences can be fraught with anxiety, rather than welcome anticipation. Unfamiliar tasks and responsibilities may create a sense of insecurity and vulnerability, especially if a wife can no longer depend on her prime source of support, her husband, and many of the responsible decisions must be made on his behalf.

The challenge was expressed this way by one wife: "I've had to learn to do a lot of things I never knew how to do before." Another woman rose to the new role:

This is where I have amazed myself, that I have been able to make decisions and accept the responsibility, because there was a farm to think about, there were responsibilities. There were money matters. There were repair bills and so forth, and I just prayed and I liked to make the decisions.

A wife who had difficulty with the new responsibilities responded:

I have to take care of all the financial business, and I have to see that everything is done. I feel like I have two jobs, you know what I mean? You can't do that.

Another wife explained her anxieties like this,

Well, you assume all responsibilities, because he's basically not thinking about the house. He's not thinking about expenses or taxes or anything else like that. When you don't really have anyone you can talk to, you get a little panicky once in a while.

Difficult decisions and new responsibilities for the wives were an undeniable outcome of their husband's placement. These challenges were either accepted as an opportunity or interpreted as formidable.

The Nursing Home

Aging has been described as a process of the loss of choice (Goldman, 1971). This portrait must be coupled with the loss of control. As this study attests, these wives had to make new adjustments and, in some cases, had little power over outcomes.

The wife who had fought to obtain "Do Not Resuscitate" (DNR) orders for her husband who had suffered several strokes and battled pneumonia, no longer had responsibility for care and therefore had to acquiesce to institutional guidelines. The tension was poignant as this woman asked rhetorically,

Would you want to live like this? If I had him at home I swear he would not be living today. If he was at home I don't think he'd live 'til morning. But they force him to live. Why? I don't think they should. What is the use of signing these Living Wills?

Her loss of power in making this critical decision was an assault on her judgement and the knowledge she had of her husband's wishes.

What these wives wanted most for their husbands was that they be comfortable. Fearful that their own death would mean the end of "monitored" care, three wives had established clear provisions in their own wills for the future care of their husbands. One wife, who visited her husband daily and had not felt that caring for him at home was any burden, said sadly,

I just hope that I will live so that I can be able to see him go before me. And after that I don't care... (crying) so that I can... What can you do? It's terrible.

Another wife, who realized she could not control the future, expressed, "I don't know what will be. I could die, right? What will be then, I don't know."

More options for security were available to the seven wives whose husbands were veterans. State-operated facilities designed for veterans protect them from being "dumped" or transferred to other nursing homes for lack of coverage or reduced benefits. The wife of one veteran addressed her plan to minimize the anxiety about their future,

> I am looking to get him back into an Illinois veteran's home, for the simple reason that if something happens to me, he will be taken care of for the rest of his life. And that's my main concern.

Establishing relationships with nursing home staff had its difficulties. Several women spoke directly of their anger and resentment about the quantity, quality, and transience of the staff, from aides to administrators. Wives spoke nostalgically of former staff that they felt had taken a personal interest in them and in the care of their husbands. One wife, a daily visitor who knew the staff well, lamented,

> It was like a family here, really. Now it's changing a lot and I feel very sorry that it is not the way it was. Because before, the head of the nurses and even the administrator, he knew us all by name. And then when he came, he'd ask, 'Mrs.D., everything ok?' And then, 'If something is wrong, tell me.' Now it is not that way. And we try to complain. And besides it is not how it used to be.

Later in the interview this woman spoke about the same issue.

> I may be angry that they are not doing more for the patients but then again it is impossible because they have not many people here working... One of these nurse's aides was always calling me "Mama"... Now she's not here anymore... There are other ones and they are disgusted because they are four, like today, four on the whole floor. And I don't know where to turn and to whom to talk. It is impossible because the patients they will suffer and they are suffering.

The wife who had complained earlier about the lack of privacy in the nursing home talked about the realities of institutional life for those who cannot afford private rooms,

> Every time I go in I sort of have to swallow a couple of times. They've taken care of him, I cannot complain about that, but it's just the idea. I resent the fact that maybe he's in the room with three other guys that are in a fetal position. They've been there about 10 - 15 years and the bad part is that he is still a little mentally alert. Not all the time, but when he is I know that he is very upset.

Another wife commented on her dissatisfaction with the placement process,

> He was basically nothing. I guess they couldn't do anymore for him. But I feel that they should have had a conference with me about it, instead of just saying, "Ok, he's going to the nursing home."

Changes which have occurred in family structure, residence and patterns of association have led more old people to live alone, and created the need for alternatives to family care, such as nursing home placement. The meaning of nursing home care varied for the women in this study. The transfer to institutional care was interpreted as a terminal destination by some: "Once you come here, that's it, that's the end". Finality was expressed by another wife who said, "I think what upsets me about this is that it's permanent -- for the rest of his life and my life too."

For others the significance of placement was expressed as relief, as they no longer had to cope with all of the everyday problems. A few of the wives said they had a sense of freedom since their husband had been placed. One woman attributed her being alive as one of the benefits of nursing home care: "Oh God, it's so great. I mean, I wouldn't be here."

Nursing home placement had its advantages. A very basic and often repeated advantage to placement was uninterrupted sleep at night. If they were not disturbed by husbands who wandered, some wives had problems sleeping because they were anxious. On the benefits of placement, one wife said, "I can sleep nights. Then, I couldn't sleep nights, I'd worry. He was starving himself. What could I do for him to eat?"

Four wives interviewed from one nursing home had created their own informal group. They often visited their husbands at the same time of the day and sat and shared this time together. All four expressed how beneficial this had been, although it had not been completely without incidents, as is part of any group process.

Love, loss, and loneliness were predictable and prominent issues. Companionship, missing most in these marriages, may account for the large amounts of time spent by these wives with their husbands at the nursing home, and may also contribute to their lack of available time to pursue other social supports. Decision making was assumed by these wives, and it was a challenge since it had formerly been shared or conceded. Apprehensions existed in regard to their monetary futures. Nursing home placement had a variety of meanings for these women, with both positive and negative consequences.

RELATIONSHIPS

The wives had a variety of emotionally supportive relationships. Eight of twelve women who had sons did not feel they could confide in them and often protected them emotionally. These wives either spoke to other women or had no one to speak to when they were depressed. This finding is consistent with a study by Matthiesen (1986), who interviewed daughters of institutionalized mothers. Typically, the sons were idealized by these mothers, but the sons rarely visited and were not a source of support to other family members.

Daughters were most often chosen as the wives' preferred source of support, although several daughters lived outside Illinois. One woman summed it up: "A daughter is a daughter. A mother is always closer to a daughter somehow." Occasionally, siblings were named as confidants. They were most often sisters who were considered to be physically well by the wife.

Friends were cultivated by the wives who created a life apart from the nursing home. One wife who was a daily visitor lamented, "Friends leave you." Friends may have been sacrificed as a lesser priority by those who were committed to daily care of their husbands in the nursing home. In many cases, both friends and relatives had died in the last year.

Relationships within the church were significant; either friendships themselves or their faith in God supported them. One woman identified her physician as her most important relationship; another woman spoke of her dog as her consistent, dependable and available companion. Another spoke of the nursing home administrator, who was always available for encouragement.

Most profound was the changed relationship with the husbands. The situation of nursing home placement forced the reality of the acuity of the husbands' illness, and yet created a sense of ambiguity for the wives. As one wife said, "When he's passed you know you've lost him." Or, "It's like a death -- like a Greek tragedy." One wife, who purposely kept her emotions from her children cried, "I'll feel tortured until he's ready to leave this earth. It's tearing me apart little bits at a time... I dread each visit." Others mourned the loss of the men they once knew: "It's like I've never been married to him. He's not the same anymore." Or, "He's not there -- not part of me anymore."

One wife stated she had not coped well with the placement. Even after five years, she was unable to accept that the relationship with her husband had changed. "It's a one-way situation -- but, we're still a couple. I've never accepted that he's not there in the same way for me." She refused to share her feelings with her sons, saying that they did not understand her need to visit their father daily. They felt that he didn't need her the way she thought he did, "I can't let them know how I feel." This woman expressed much gratitude after the interview and said it was the first time she had talked about her feelings in such depth.

Wives' relationships with husbands, sons and friends suffered as a result of placement. When daughters were available they were often the chosen confidant.

The coding category of <u>relationships</u> dealt primarily with loss. Although no startling revelations were found, the wives' responses were noteworthy. Some relatives had died. Some friends had also died. Others had friends who were apathetic. Family, marital, and supportive relationships were damaged by illness and placement.

In a sense, the wives had been replaced in their role as primary caregivers by the nursing home staff. On a literal and yet visceral level, aspects of the marital relationship had been lost or transferred. The husband was now shared with a more or less impersonal group of people who were often without the benefit of his or the family's history. The essence of the relatedness was changed by the nature of a more public environment.

Loss of the past, in the memory of the person the husband once was, combined with a loss of plans for the future, dealt a hard emotional blow to the wives. These circumstances had not been anticipated. As one wife disappointedly recounted,

> I get scared at times, because all of a sudden you are old and you don't realize it. The years went by and we wasted so much time with illness and him being sick. We used to plan we'd be traveling, and we couldn't.

The loss of plans was painfully expressed by one wife in response to what she missed most about the relationship;

> Having him. And the pain of seeing him down like that. He enjoyed life to the fullest. He had plans. He always says, "I'll never live long enough to do all the things that I wanted to do." But we'd walk around that farm together and he'd say, "I'm going to do this, and I'm going to... He was going to build a chapel on the farm. He was going to build that. And always... Well, still, he hasn't given up. He hasn't given up.

Hope was lost to a grim reality for this wife and for others.

PERSPECTIVES / FEELINGS

Love

Wives were asked if they had cared for their husbands at home out of a) duty and obligation, b) love, c) reciprocity, d) guilt, or e) because there was no one else. Love for their husband was the most common feeling expressed by these wives. Caregiving was motivated primarily by love and less by duty or a sense of obligation. The desire to nurture and give care was expressed by the wife who stated "I always wanted to do all I could for him." She cared for her husband at home for seven years. His depression and seclusion prevented her from hiring outside help. Several attempts were made to hire in-home help, but her husband drove them away.

A woman whose family told her she should not spend all her time at the nursing home replied, "It's true in a way, because it doesn't help." When asked why she did come every day, she responded,

'Cause I love him! I tell them you can't be married to a man for all these years, you cannot have three children and just dump him. That's the way I put it.

The hardship of chronic illness took its toll on one relationship. The wife of an alcoholic voiced her ambivalence, "Before it was love. Now I don't know what it is."

With one exception, all the wives asserted they had had happy marriages based on love. Relationships built on love and longevity, as indicated by the respondents in this study, may have made it possible to endure and accept the unfortunate events that developed later in the marriage.

Loss

As people age they tend to accumulate the kinds of deficits that impair their support systems. For the wives in this study the compounded losses included significant aspects of their relationships with their husbands and others, control over certain caregiving responsibilities, income, health and mobility, a lifestyle, and loss of dreams for the future. Many had lost their sense of freedom as they felt obliged to frequently monitor their husbands' placement. The losses tended to isolate them from the contacts necessary to forestall feelings of loneliness.

Loneliness

The "empty house" was a significant theme expressed by the women in this study. One wife whose husband was still mentally alert put it this way,

Oh... the companionship. The house is so lonesome and empty, especially in the evening and in the morning when I get up. Right away the radio goes on. You've got to have something talking.

In response to the inquiry about what new problems developed since placement, she said, "I am always by myself, that is the problem." For the wives who live alone there was potential for both desolation and isolation. Habits and attachments over many years of marriage were disrupted by the separation of nursing home placement.

One woman only saw her son once a year, as he lived in another state. She was troubled by the difficult relationship she had with her daughter-in-law;

> If I complain too much, my daughter-in-law tells me off. I guess she don't think my attitude is right... I have a nice apartment and I have nice furniture, and I tell her, "You don't have to tell me I have nice things." I feel that they could call me sometime (voice breaking), but they are busy with their own lives and their own kids.

If her family could not be counted on for support, she had little choice but to adopt a personal stance of self-reliance. Feelings of loneliness were related to issues of dependency. It was difficult for these wives to ask for or accept assistance from friends or family, whether concrete, financial, or emotional.

Guilt

When the wives were asked directly if they felt bound to care for their spouse out of guilt, they often denied feeling guilty of anything. However, in the course of the interview, they would share that they were touched by guilt on occasion. A wife who sought professional help for herself and her husband said,

> I don't feel guilty of anything. But once in awhile you get the feeling that you are guilty. But counselors always told me, "You did 100% for this man."

When asked how the placement affected her emotionally, one wife responded,

> I guess in a way I feel a little guilty. I keep thinking, you know, bring him home and take care of him. But I wouldn't he able to handle it seven days a week.

Realizing the enormity of the care her husband required helped to relieve her doubts and potential self-blame.

Another wife did experience guilt great enough to cause a depressive reaction, and she underwent hospitalization;

After I put him in the nursing home I felt very guilty. And I got to the point where I just didn't care about anything anymore. My daughter saw it. She took me to the doctor and I was in the hospital under psychiatric help.

Evidently, this woman recovered from both her guilt and her depression. Her parting comment to the interviewer was, "I am happier now than I have ever been."

Guilt was minimized by these wives. They had been able to justify to themselves and to others that placement was acceptable. The occasional pangs of guilt which were expressed were connected to an autistic desire to bring their husbands home and assume their former position as primary caregiver.

STRATEGIES FOR COPING

Anticipatory Grief and Bereavement

Responses of most wives in the present study were similar to those of older widows described by Hill, Thompson, and Gallagher, (1988). Both groups engaged in "spontaneous rehearsal," discussions of preparations such as funeral arrangements, considerations regarding financial security, feelings about being left behind, and ruminations about what the future would be like if the spouse died before the respondent. Despite the desire, there was little hope that the husband would improve or that he would return home. Anticipatory bereavement can be imposed by nursing home placement. The reflections and behavior of some of the wives indicated an acceptance of the probable death of their husbands.

Avoidance

A contrast to anticipatory bereavement was the coping strategy of taking "one day at a time." Rather than to plan for the future, there was conscious avoidance of what was to come. This orientation to the present was a familiar pattern which helped them in their efforts to achieve control over a painful and predictable outcome, the death of their spouse.

Denial of thoughts about the future was categorized as coping through avoidance. Affective statements by the wives indicated how they felt about themselves, their marriages, and their futures. The wives' statements were "preconscious." They revealed persistent feelings which periodically slipped into consciousness but were quickly suppressed or denied. Thoughts of the future were too frightening or too painful to contemplate. A common response was, "I never think about the future," or "I don't want to think about it." These remarks reflected the wives efforts to ignore thoughts about the ramifications of their husband's death.

Several wives denied the burdens of caregiving at home, despite years of caring for husbands who were quite debilitated. Most minimized the difficulties, stating that they preferred to be caregivers. Two wives were remarkable in their characterizations of what amounted to 24 hours a day of caregiving. When asked directly, "What were the burdens of caring for your husband at home," one woman responded, "It was a wonderful time, really. I never did anything so fulfilling." This wife and her husband had two adopted children and were quite religious. Her descriptions of actual caregiving made her statements seem paradoxical. Her days were consumed with the total care of her husband, who had suffered a stroke. He was still able to communicate with her and was verbally and physically abusive and demanding. In the morning she would toilet him, change the linens, give him breakfast, bathe him, and then administer physical therapy. It was then midday, and she would prepare his lunch and wash the dishes. If he napped, she might have respite in the afternoon. Before the evening meal, she would exercise him at the bedside. Nights were the worst, as he would often cry out in pain and keep her awake. Any free moments she had to herself, she used to pray.

Another wife had grown up in Norway. Her husband, an Alzheimer's patient, was from Sweden. She negated any sense of difficulty: "I didn't feel that it was any burden." Her sense of the future had been lost, "I don't even think about it anymore." Her husband no longer recognized her and kept her up at night with his wandering behavior. A very large man, he was difficult to handle physically. Although she had two sons, she derived most of her support from an Alzheimer's family support group.

Several explanations are offered for the discrepancy between the difficult situation and the denial of the burden by these wives. Perhaps the perception is reality, and the 24-hour caregiving was truly not a burden. In retrospect, it may not have been a burden, as the wives now experienced some respite with their husbands' transfer to the nursing home. To support the perspective that the reality of the experience was not a burden, one could surmise that for these wives, the rewards of self-sacrifice were sufficient. Their statements gave meaning to their relationships and reflected their willingness to sacrifice. The wives' statements overtly denied any burden associated with the management of their husbands' total care, suggesting that the wives needed to maintain an image, to the interviewer as well as to themselves, of being "all-giving."

For some, avoidance was a conscious choice, a mechanism to counteract depressive thoughts. Avoidance of thoughts about their husbands' condition and future were manifest in statements about how they "keep on pushing" or "help others." Several women were active with part-time jobs, ran errands for others, pursued social contacts, or immersed themselves in housework. Several wives deliberately used books or television to distract themselves from thoughts about their husbands.

Helping behavior reflected a model of caregiving that, for some, extended beyond the husband to include other relatives, neighbors, and occasionally other residents in the nursing home. These women derived satisfaction knowing they made a positive difference in someone else's life.

In addition to visiting her husband three times a week, one wife spent a lot of time helping her brother-in-law. She good-humoredly reported,

> T.'s brother is 90 years old and he has such a hard time walking... So this morning I took him shopping and I took him to the bank and I took him to pay his insurance... Thank goodness I drive! (laugh)

This woman received immediate gratitude from her brother-in-law on these excursions. Her husband, a victim of Alzheimer's disease, was unable to express any meaningful sentiments.

One wife, who was a daily visitor at the nursing home, bemoaned her inability to provide direct help to others. Her monetary contributions to charity were her way of assisting those less fortunate.

Use of Self

The use of self as a coping tool was defined as conscious awareness of what one is doing or the ability to regard the self in action (Middleman, 1983). Emphasized here are self-monitoring, identification of thoughts, wishes, and feelings, as well as problem-solving. Other procedures involved self-instructions and self-assessment. These cognitive approaches involved personal appraisal and were categorized as adaptive coping strategies.

Most wives had positive outlooks on life. Several women clearly identified themselves as "positive thinkers." Throughout her marriage, one wife indicated, all the decisions had been left to her:

I'm a positive thinker. I find something good about every day... You have these problems, you have to solve them, whatever they might be. And I did it, I did what I had to do.

Positive thinking was associated with a competent image of herself which aided her in her ability to make decisions and solve problems.

The problems of placement were accepted by some wives and this acceptance was reinforced with self-instructions. As one wife, who cared for her husband at home for five years before her husband was placed, said, "It's just something you have to accept. There is no sense sitting here moping and saying why did it happen to me." This woman was so busy visiting her husband and caring for others that she "didn't have time to feel lonely." Her involvement with others suggested an active coping style. She would not indulge in self-pity and demonstrated a commitment to go on with her life. Her activity and acceptance seemed to reflect her adjustment to the placement of her husband.

One woman's husband had been ill since their marriage. His injuries were the result of an accident in World War II. According to the wife, they had both adapted quite well and worked together in a small business. Her philosophy, which had supported her in the past, seemed to be failing,

> I have always had a good outlook on life. If today isn't so good, tomorrow will be better. And I still have that, but it doesn't seem to work that way for me lately.

A positive attitude mirrored an inner strength that motivated these women in times of adversity. Self-reliance was shown by the wife who attributed her ability to cope to herself, "Who else is there?" This woman had no family support other than a son who lived far away. Her coping style was also one of keeping busy. Relatively younger than the other wives, she continued to work part-time and managed daily visits to her husband. She described herself as "sort of independent."

The group setting of the nursing home provided constant exposure to those who were more debilitated or impaired than these wives' husbands. Some wives used comparative self-monitoring in order to gauge a comfortable or appropriate degree of self-indulgence. One example was the comment by the wife who had lived with her husband's illness throughout the duration of the marriage, "I'm not feeling sorry for myself. I know a lot of people are worse off than we are."

By virtue of traditional marriages, many wives had depended on their husbands to handle problems and make decisions. Over time, the husbands gradually withdrew from these responsibilities due to illness and the wives' compensatory capabilities were challenged. Lifelong coping techniques such as positive thinking helped these women adjust to new responsibilities and lifestyles.

Family Support

Only half of the participants in this study indicated that the family was the base of most support. The definition of family included sons, daughters, sisters, nieces, nephews, the husband's family and in- laws. Support included emotional reinforcement, financial assistance, and assistance with tasks and errands which included transportation. Support also included social companionship and care when the wives were sick.

One woman had two sons but neither was a source of support. One daughter-in-law who lived nearby had consistently rejected her when she exhibited any emotional dependency. This was a great disappointment to the wife whose only other relatives lived in Europe. Occasionally she would call her sister abroad and pour her heart out. However, the cost prohibited her from calling often. An Alzheimer's family support group was the primary source of support.

Another wife had several children. Her son, however, refused to visit his father in the nursing home as it was too painful. This woman spent hours daily with her husband. She advised her family that if they wanted to see her, they would have to visit her at the nursing home. As a result, the mother/son relationship was damaged. Interestingly, this wife stated that her doctor was the source of greatest support.

One wife who had a daughter by a previous marriage was quick to say that her support was derived from the friend who accompanied her to the interview. Originally, the "friend" had been sent as a home health aide by an agency to assist the wife with her husband. He was extremely difficult to manage due to his uncooperative and, at times, violent behavior. The home health aide befriended the wife and realized she needed more help in order to maintain her husband at home. Eight years ago, the aide voluntarily began to spend her days off with this couple until one and a half years ago when the husband entered the nursing home. Although the wife was close to her daughter, she felt that a special friendship had developed between her and the aide. Caring together for this man had created a special bond. This friend was her most valuable source of support.

In two separate cases, children attempted to give support to their mothers by sending them on vacations. In one instance the plan backfired. Just as the mother arrived at her destination on the west coast, she received a telephone call from her daughter, who had taken the responsibility of caring for her father while her mother was away. The father was reported missing. Shortly afterward he was located, but had battered his daughter as she attempted to help him into her car. The mother flew home immediately. The experience was an eye-opener for the daughter, who gained a greater understanding of the dangers and difficulties of caring for an Alzheimer's victim. This incident led to family support for the husband's placement.

Most women felt they could not take a vacation because they could not depend on other family members to take their place as monitors in the nursing home. Their commitments to their husbands through marriage made their relationships special. They felt that the care and vigilance they gave their spouse could not be expected of someone else, even a relative. Realistically, few other relatives had the time which would permit daily visits, or visits even three times a week. Jobs and family responsibilities prevented them from being available for relief and respite to the wives.

Other family members were sometimes available when there were no children. The geographic mobility of the children meant that some families were separated by distance. When the expectation for support from the family was not forthcoming, the disappointment was visible, as many women cried at these points in the interview. When families were not available as resources, friends, support groups, and a physician were substituted.

Professional Help

Professional help was sought by seven wives in an effort to cope with the emotional aspects of placement. Designated as professional care were counseling, psychiatry, and support groups. Prior to permanent placement only a few husbands had professional care at home. Services included adult day care, visiting nurses, and home health aides, and, in one case, nursing home as respite was arranged on weekends. With one exception, attempts to involve home care services were unsuccessful. The aggressive behavior of the husbands thwarted efforts of health care professionals and the wives were left again as the sole providers of care.

Religion

Religion was practiced by sixteen of the wives as a strategy for coping. Prayer and other practices of faith were significant aspects of their lives. Much of the wives' ability to persevere was attributed to their "faith in the Lord."

On numerous occasions throughout the interviews, wives depicted their situations, past and present, as in the hands of God. This would suggest that, for the majority of women studied, the locus of control was external.

Humor

There was little opportunity to explore humor as a coping mechanism, due to the serious nature of the questions. In hindsight, humor should have been a probe incorporated into the questionnaire. Several wives volunteered that their sense of humor was a factor in their ability to cope with their husband's illness and placement. "You have to laugh," one woman said, and proceeded to tell a story which was both tragic and comic. At mealtime at the nursing home, the trays were set up in front of those residents who, presumably, could feed themselves. One day, as this wife looked up from feeding her husband, she saw a resident with his face in his plate. This pathetic picture was, at the same time, uproariously funny. It reminded her of a scene from a Mel Brooks movie.

The husband with dementia who dressed himself in his wife's lingerie created a hilarious scene which allowed her to laugh at the ridiculous situation. Some of the unwitting behaviors of those who are confused are humorous.

Wishful Thinking

Wishful thinking referred to the coping strategy which provided six wives with an escape from the pain of reality. The autistic hope they projected was a fantasy which focused on their husbands' coming home and included hoping "for a miracle" and wishing they could "change what happened" or the way they felt.

SUMMARY

Coping strategies used by the wives included anticipatory bereavement, avoidance of the future, use of self, family and professional help, religion, humor, and wishful thinking. This sample of wives displayed active involvement with their husbands, a way to manage their feelings associated with lost aspects of the marital relationship.

Wives either engaged in anticipatory bereavement or avoided the future in efforts to manage their feelings of uncertainty. Two categories of emotional functioning emerged -- those wives who were positive thinkers and those who were depressed. The wives who were depressed were more likely to avoid thoughts or behaviors oriented to the future.

THE UNEXPECTED FINDING - ABUSE BY THE HUSBAND

In this study, older wives had been caregivers for their debilitated husbands an average of eight years before their husbands were placed in a nursing home. In accord with the evaluation of stress as a motivation for abuse, one would expect some of the wives to have been abusers of their husbands. On the contrary, half the wives had been victims of abuse by their husbands. In one case, a wife struck back after her husband initiated physical attacks, This same wife returned verbal insults as well. Definitions of abuse have been vague in prior studies. This research studied two aspects of abuse, physical and verbal, defined in this way:

Physical abuse was categorized by an adapted scale of violence created by Straus (1979) and defined by attacks which resulted in harm to the body.

Type A. Acts of Minor Violence Type B. Acts of Severe Violence
  1. Threw something   4. Kicked/bit/hit with fist
  2. Pushed/grabbed/shoved   5. Hit/tried to hit with something
  3. Slapped   6. Beat up

Verbal abuse included threats of harm, intimidations, disparaging remarks, insults, and cursing. An attack by words constituted verbal abuse. Any objective measurement of psychological harm resulting from physical and verbal abuse was beyond the scope of this project. The study was not designed to measure the incidence of abuse among elderly wives. However, during the first interview abuse was revealed. The direct question of abuse by their mate was included in all subsequent interviews.

Twelve husbands cared for at home by their wives prior to nursing home placement were found to be physically or verbally abusive. This behavior was associated with the husband's illness and was attributed to the husband's loss of control over his environment.

These findings support speculation that the husband's illness may signal loss of control, which leads to a sense of powerlessness, and hence, violent, aggressive behavior toward their wives. A wife of a polio victim theorized about his behavior prior to placement: "He was losing control of his life. He <u>had</u> to fight back."

If the stress and dependency theories are applied to the wives, they would have been expected to abuse their dependent husbands. The unrelenting responsibilities of caregiving (an average of eight years) included coping with alcohol abuse by two husbands, wandering, falls, incontinence, and verbal as well as physical attacks. Most wives handled all the affairs and financial dealings of the household; for many, this meant acquiring new skills. The support of their mate was no longer available. This complex mix of internal and external stressors created a situation in which abuse toward their husbands could be expected. Only one wife struck back at her husband. For her, nursing home placement was the only way to halt the cycle of violence.

Perhaps the stress and dependence theories are less applicable to the marital relationship than they are to adult children with elderly parents. The wives did feel some inversion of the responsibilities, but they clearly needed to preserve and protect the integrity of their marriage. They accepted and rationalized their husbands' behavior. Their devotion to the memory of the man they once knew took precedence over thoughts of inflicting pain.

TABLE II - FREQUENCY OF ABUSE BY DIAGNOSIS

Respondent	Type of Abuse	Husband's Illness	Length of Home Caregiving
001	Verbal	Depression	6.5 years
002	Physical (struck)	Alzheimer's	4
004	Physical/Verbal "3 times attempted to strangle her, "kicked", "beat up"	Alzheimer's	4
006	Physical/Verbal "Threw furniture"	Alcoholism/ Alzheimer's	7.5
007	Physical/Verbal swearing, threats, combative threw and broke things	Alzheimer's	7
008	Physical/Verbal swearing, physical threats, struck out at her	Stroke	2.5
011	Physical/Verbal "whacked us with fists", "knocked me down", strangled her, verbal threat to kill	Alzheimer's	1
013	Physical mutual hitting	Stroke	1
017	Verbal	Stroke	9 mos.
019	"Probably abusive but forgot what was said"	Alzheimer's	6
021	Verbal	Polio	3.5
024	Physical/Verbal threatened, battered	Alcoholism/ Alzheimer's	19

In nursing home placement, separation of the ill and abusive husband from the caregiver wife was achieved. In several of these cases, the husband continued to be abusive in the nursing home. The recipient was generally the staff of nurses and aides. For a few husbands, the behavior ceased altogether in the nursing home.

The primary theories of elderly abuse do not refer to or account for the results found in this study. Studies which have examined the symptoms and effects of Alzheimer's disease recognize the aggressive and abusive tendencies of these patients. Alzheimer's victims are not responsible for their behavior, but the potential for danger clearly exists.

Five of the twelve husbands in this study who were described as abusive did not have diagnoses of Alzheimer's disease; they suffered from stroke, alcoholism, depression, and polio. Except for two husbands who had been alcoholic, all of the incidents of abuse were identified as occurring with the onset of the husband's illness. The abused wives did redefine the behavior of their husbands, and with inner strength, positive thinking, faith and the history of a highly satisfying marriage they were able to provide long-term home care prior to institutionalization.

UNPLANNED CLINICAL ISSUES VS. GOALS OF THE RESEARCH

Data were included on one wife who was too distraught to complete the instruments, but what she volunteered was rich material. Her husband had recently been placed in the nursing home. Her experience illustrates that the period of adjustment takes place in the first three months of placement. Two follow-up calls were made to her as my concerns were: 1) that she seek professional help for apparent depression, and 2) to determine whether or not she was able to complete the interview at another time. She had obtained the name of a psychiatrist and planned to call for an appointment. She declined, however, to be interviewed further: "The questions are too painful. These are all the things I am trying to forget."

Although the interview was not finished, her responses are included in the study as her contribution was considered significant. As her husband had been placed less than three months prior to the interview, it is likely that sufficient time had not passed and the crisis pervaded. She was evidently depressed, as she cried throughout the interview and spoke of her inability to function or seek help. At this time she had not adjusted to the placement of her husband. She denied having any prior depressive episodes. This experience lent support to the decision to interview only those wives whose husbands had been placed for a minimum of three months.

It is possible that she may never adapt to the placement as other wives have. This wife was also the only respondent who projected a sense of mediocrity about the quality of her marriage: "It was average." In a study of widows (Flaherty et al., 1987), those who had felt their marriages to be successful were those most well-adjusted to the loss of their spouse. If the results of the study of widows are applied to this group of wives who call themselves "married widows", poor marital adjustment may be indicative of poor adjustment to placement. Unfortunately, this wife did not complete the Marital-Adjustment Scale.

THE ROLE OF THE INTERVIEWER

"Field work, like any interaction of everyday life, evokes the whole range of feelings associated with everyday life. Transference is evoked mainly through talking with others". (C.A.B. Warren, 1988)

As I explored gender issues in field research in the literature, I became clearly aware of my own counter-transference with respondents when I asked them to share their personal history and experience. What would I do in a similar situation of illness and abuse? I found myself identifying with these wives and yet separating myself historically, socially, politically, and emotionally. Would the next generation of women continue their marital commitment in this type of relationship?

The bulk of the interviews were transcribed by one other person and I was curious as to whether she had experienced any of the same feelings. She was skeptical of the "positive attitudes" which most wives expressed that they tried to maintain. She felt that many of the wives were guilty and angry and not honest in their reality.

It would appear that the researcher's acceptance of the wives' responses as positive, adaptive, and reliable is related to her investment in the study which is undeniable. It may also be affected by the personal process of the interviewing itself. However, the reader is referred to Wiseman's rules (p. 27) which support the wives subjective assessment as their reality.

SUMMARY

The wives' perspectives on nursing home placement included feelings of love for their husband and loneliness; they characterized themselves as married widows. Most felt they needed money; they were burdened by bills and dwindled savings.

Religion was a dominant coping mechanism for the Catholic and Protestant wives; less so for the Jewish wives. The wives either planned and actively prepared for the future or avoided thoughts or plans related to the future. Those who had interests, friends, and activities outside of the nursing home expressed their ability to accept and cope with the circumstances. The wives who made plans for the future were also in positions which better prepared them for the inevitable death of their mate.

The wives who were actively engaged in anticipatory bereavement were less depressed than those who coped by living "day by day." According to the results of the CES-D Scale, half of the respondents were depressed. More than half alluded to their struggles with depressive episodes. Most women cried at some point during the interview. The wives expressed little guilt; so much time was invested as primary caregivers.

The incidence of reported abuse by a majority of wives was a surprise finding. Contrary to the literature on violence against the elderly, the perpetrator was the ill husband. Clinical experience with Alzheimer's patients supports that this behavior can be expected. However, only seven abusive husbands in the study had Alzheimer's, two of them with secondary diagnoses of alcoholism. The diagnoses of the five other abusive husbands included stroke, polio and depression. The wives held that the abuse was related to the illness. This conclusion separated the painful incidents from the person who inflicted them.

Although in good physical health, the wives felt that the stress of their husbands' placement was a factor in their own emotional health. It was especially difficult for those who visited daily and who had little support from their families. Often family members, especially children, did not understand the needs of these wives to demonstrate such devotedness to their husbands, who were often unresponsive.

Fifteen of the twenty-four women indicated their income was "inadequate"; several deplored the lack of federal or other support for long-term care. Four felt their financial futures to be bleak.

Those who visited every day were often exhausted and had no energy to perform household tasks. Their eating habits suffered: "Too tired to eat," they would say. Fatigue, lack of appropriate nutrition and withdrawn family support were chronic issues for the daily visitors. Other wives visited an average of three times a week.

Religion was a major source of support to the wives. Many women were stoic and accepting; however, their vigilance of their husbands' care in the nursing home took precedence over other aspects of their lives. Missing most for the wives was companionship, intimacy, and communication with their mate, especially for those whose husbands no longer recognized them. Many had not had a vacation in years. Some said they had never had one. None would consider a vacation as long as their husband was in the nursing home. Most wives expressed their need to provide for the future care of their husbands in the event of the wife's illness or death, or else they prayed for a merciful death for their husband while they were still alive.

The women "did it all" in terms of the inherited responsibilities. In many cases, they also carried the emotional burden of a "one-way" marriage. Unrequited love of sorts was sustained by the wives' demonstrated commitment to their husbands.

All of the women characterized themselves in ambiguous terms regarding their role as wives since their husbands were transferred to the nursing home. The expression "married widows" is descriptive of how they perceived themselves and their situation.

TABLE III - PROFILE OF WIVES

Category	Mean Response
Average Age:	72
Living Situation:	Lives alone
Employment:	Retired, had previously been in a service or factory position.
Education:	High School graduate
Religion:	Practices religion, strong faith, factor in coping
Ethnicity:	Eastern European extraction
Average Income:	$12,000 per year
Physical Health:	Good

TABLE IV - PROFILE OF HUSBANDS

Category	Mean Response
Illnesses Include:	Depression, stroke, Alzheimer's, alcoholism, ALS, MS and polio
Average Length of Illness:	Eight years
Problems Prior to Placement:	Paranoia, hallucinations, wandering, physical and verbal abuse, demanding 24 hour care
Average Length of Time in Nursing Home:	One year
Descriptions of Husband's Current Situation:	Incontinence, wheelchair or bedbound, not communicative

TABLE V - PROFILE OF MARRIAGE

Category	Mean Response
Average Length of Marriage:	45 years
Description of Marriage Before Illness:	Very Good
Description of Marriage Before Placement:	"Very emotional", "Getting hard", "Not good"
Description of Marriage Now:	"I don't have 'a marriage - It's shattered", "I feel like a widow , "It's nothing","I'm married but I don't have a husband"
Perspective on Future:	"I don't think about it", "I live day by day"
Missing Most:	Companionship, communication
Needs:	Financial

COMPARISON OF FINDINGS

Coping refers to efforts to master conditions of harm, threat or challenge, when a routine or automatic response is not readily available. Environmental demands must be met with new behavioral solutions or old ones must be adapted to meet the current stress (White, 1974). Successful coping involves securing adequate information and the ability to problem-solve and adapt under relatively difficult conditions. Personality attributes and situational elements are involved in the process of coping. Situational elements include the social and emotional supports which sustain us by giving comfort.

Questions regarding coping and depression were included on the instruments and on the questionnaire. Similar questions did not always evoke similar responses from the wives. The discrepancies may have resulted from: ambivalent feelings of the wives, discomfort with the interview process and/or the interviewer, inadequacy of the instruments or inadequacy of the questionnaire. The last explanation would seem the least likely, as the questionnaire was designed with probes to elicit depth and promote clarification. Perhaps if the instruments had been administered first and the questionnaire followed, the interviewer would have had the opportunity to explore apparent discrepancies.

The wives were grouped into two categories depending on their ability to cope with the adversity of unplanned events by making changes and adjustments in their relationships, lifestyles, and routines. Seven wives were identified as positive copers, seven as poor copers. The balance of wives fell between these two categories. None had escaped the challenge of adjustment; As one wife aptly said, "We're under the constant stress of this situation."

The seven wives identified as positive copers indicated that they had coped successfully consistently throughout their lives. Their ability to adapt was ascribed to their "inner strength." They utilized: 1) professional help (counselors, psychiatrists, and self-help groups); 2) religion; 3) self-reliance; 4) humor; and 5) work.

Poor copers volunteered that they were not coping well and expressed emotional lability as well as vulnerability, due to lack of support from family or friends. Denial was also evident in the avoidance of emotion as a way of suppressing affect. These wives negated the reality of tremendous physical and emotional strain.

The cumulative effects of loss and change on some older people gives them a history of survival. On the other hand, at this stage in life there are often fewer resources to alleviate the older person's increasing concrete and emotional needs.

The distinguishing characteristic of the two groups of wives was the positive copers' ability to detach from their husbands in the nursing home through work, religion, humor, professional help, or their own inner resolve. It would be interesting to compare these two groups later as widows. Do the positive copers continue to fare as well?

The poor copers were apt to be daily visitors, still consumed by their husbands' caregiving needs. They spoke openly of their emotional dependence on the marital relationship, despite, in most cases, the husband's inability to reciprocate. They were bereft of family support. Over half of the poor copers had significant health problems.

The positive copers had better physical health and were motivated to use their positive attitude to social advantage. They were more capable of pursuing a job, friends, or hobbies. They could "allow" themselves to be separated from their husbands without the guilt that prevented the poor copers from time and life apart from their institutionalized spouse.

CONCLUSIONS

Three issues pertinent to the area of gerontology emerged from this study: caregiving, abuse, and nursing home placement. The discussion which follows will explore the implications of the findings and their relationship to these issues. Clinical, policy, educational, and research recommendations for the field of social work follow this section.

Findings indicate that this sample of women had cared for their spouse eight years prior to placement. Long-term caregiving at home was accepted as part of their role as wives. Over half of the sample were in domestic situations in which they were vulnerable to verbal and physical expressions of abuse by an invalid husband.

Lack of awareness and acceptance on the part of other family members, especially children, contributed to the wives' burden. The extent of caregiving performed by the wife and the incidence of abusive behavior by the husband was negatively related to the assistance from others.

A prevalent post-placement theme was insecurity about the financial future. This, coupled with role ambiguity, precipitated a depressive reaction, especially when the husband's recovery was unlikely.

Depression following placement of the husband afflicted half of the women in this sample. The problem of depression also went undetected by family members and friends. The other side of family denial or acceptance had to do with the problems these women had with disclosure. They deliberately "protected" others from information about abuse, depression, or money, because they felt these problems might be "disturbing" to family or friends.

Lack of reports on the prevalence of elder abuse has been attributed to under-reporting; families are reluctant to report incidences of violence. The assumption that elder abuse is not common reflects problems in definition, concept, and methodology. In addition, the literature is sparse in reference to cause and intervention.

The author did not expect to find that half of the wives reported instances of verbal and physical abuse by their ill husbands. The wives' willingness to discuss this issue was unexpected as well.

It is with some caution that the husbands' behavior is termed abusive, which implies intent to do harm. Although the definition of

75

abusive behavior in this study was not denied by the wives, they did separate it and associate it with loss of control due to their husbands' physical and emotional illness. The need for clarification and definition cannot be minimized. However, the women were at risk of and encountered physical and emotional injury.

The results reveal a profile of a long-time caregiver who is emotionally isolated and who clings to the threads of an indefinable, elusive marriage. She has defined herself in part, by her commitment and involvement in her husband's care. However, her caregiving role as a wife seems to change once her husband is placed. The wife's identity as caregiver was diminished after the husband's transfer. Sharing the caregiver role with the institution relieved some of the physically exhausting aspects of giving care and lessened the threat of assault, but also lessened the direct time spent in meaningful tasks of the marriage essential to the relationship and personal identity of the wife; for example, the responsibility and expectation of meal preparation, and the intimacy of sleeping together. These findings suggest a need for identification and clinical intervention with elderly wives who have served as caregivers.

IMPLICATIONS FOR CLINICAL PRACTICE, POLICY, EDUCATION AND RESEARCH

According to Moss and Halmandaris (1977), about half of the elderly who are institutionalized come from another facility and the other half are admitted from home. Both the hospital and the nursing home provide fertile opportunities for social workers to assess the home environment, family supports, and emotional stability of a spouse who has been a caregiver and struggles with the issues of placement.

CLINICAL PRACTICE

Hospital discharge planning of patients to nursing homes can be improved by educating social workers, as well as family members, to be sensitive to the clinical issues and concrete needs expressed by the wives in this study: lack of in-home family support, abuse, depression, and lack of finances. When the unacceptable idea of nursing home placement becomes a reality, support must be given to those who experience the changes.

The meaning of the changes are paramount. Nursing home placement was interpreted by some wives as a defeat. It was an indication to them that they could no longer be the sole provider of care for their ill husbands. Empathic support and acceptance by the social worker of the family's decision to place is essential for them to feel comfortable in their choice.

Social workers in the nursing home are in key positions to structure support groups for wives and family members of residents. Issues of transition, loss, role ambiguity, and loneliness, as well as legal or financial problems and coping with the future can be addressed. Shared advice and experience from those in similar situations have been shown to be effective and is a basic tenet of self-help groups.

A formal support group could be maintained to:

A. Offer companionship and emotional encouragement;

B. Provide resource information and educative programs which address the wives' new burdens and responsibilities (for example, selling a home, obtaining durable power of attorney);

C. Reduce the stress of added responsibilities through relaxation exercises;

D. Develop a satisfaction scale which measures the success of these interventions.

Social workers in community geriatric settings should be alert to this high risk group and to creative interventions that center on education and program development. Geriatric assessment clinics, wellness centers, adult day care programs and outpatient ambulatory care settings are examples of sites which could benefit from the implications of this study.

Abuse against elderly women is as serious as any kind of elder abuse identified in the literature, primarily because women are easily physically dominated by men. The potential risk of harm is therefore greater. In a study by Pillemer and Finklehor (1988), emotional forms of psychological abuse (verbal threats, insults and attacks) are often perceived as more damaging by women than are similar insults directed at men by women. Men were found to be more impervious to both physical and verbal attacks.

A social work assessment which includes a "detection" protocol of domestic abuse would be a preliminary to intervention. Social workers should take an active role in discussing the stresses of chronic disease, feelings of anger and shame, and the burdens of physically and emotionally demanding care.

In this study the question was asked directly, "Has your husband ever abused you verbally or physically?" There were no adverse reactions to this pointed inquiry. If the response was "yes", then further probing followed in regard to frequency and precipitating circumstances.

This study challenges the assumption in the literature that caregivers of the impaired are at risk to become abusive. The importance of this assumption is not to be denied. Rather than viewing the results of this study in contrast to prior studies, it would be key to realize the clinical importance of assessing potential and actual abuse in the caregiving dyad. Social workers, as well as other health care professionals, should be sensitive to the subtle ways these cases may present themselves; for example, frequent readmissions to the hospital.

Once an assessment is made, intervention, follow-up and prevention should be implemented. However, as O'Malley, Segal and Perez (1979) have discovered, 40% of allegedly abused elderly refuse further evaluation and intervention. None in this study were referred to social service agencies. Ideally, the best time to intervene is before abuse happens. Occasionally, we are confronted with an ethical dilemma. We must respect people's rights to privacy, while striving to achieve their maximum health and comfort. This right includes the right to refuse interventions. Refusal of services may stem from a person's fear of losing independence, embarrassment over the current state of the relationship and fear of institutionalization. Keeping a marriage may be less threatening.

Statutes in some states require mandatory reporting of abuse. The report of abuse without prior consent of the family could present tremendous difficulties. The violence in the cases described in this study was not defined by the victims as a crime. Unfortunately, the legislative response to the political issue of abuse of the elderly has developed without the benefit of any systematic analysis of theories of causation, study of potential interventions and their risks and benefits, or appreciation of the ethical dilemmas confronting practitioners. Future studies of abuse which cite the vulnerability of the elderly will be useful for identifying a population at risk, and for promoting interventions that will reduce the likelihood of violence.

Supportive services should be suggested. For example, advice and referral regarding support groups and opportunities for respite care can be given. The families who use brief nursing home placement as respite are more inclined to find long-term placement more acceptable (Given, Collins, and King, 1989). Pillemer (1985) has suggested the development of shelters for older women, support groups for this group, and financial aid to set up independent living programs.

Within the nursing home, policy makers and administrators need to work together to make respite care readily available for any older person and their caregiver who is in need of such support. The options are currently available only for those who can afford to pay privately. Pursuing Medicaid and Medicare reimbursement for respite care will work to create a more equitable allocation of resources.

Grants to fund programs for community organizations have potential on local and national levels for assisting the elderly and their caregivers. Through an organization of churches, volunteers could be available to provide transportation, companionship and respite care. Similar services at little or no cost are currently provided for many seniors through community programs such as the Department on Aging. However, these services are virtually impossible to arrange at night and on weekends. Most of the women in this study were religious but felt disconnected from their place of worship and their religious community, due to lack of transportation and inability to leave their husbands unattended.

On a national level, the development of a service sector, such as a youth corps, modeled after several western european countries and smaller scale pilot enterprises in the U.S., would help overcome some of these difficulties. The program would obligate a person to donate a year of service to the country, doing various tasks in exchange for living expenses or a year of college tuition. From a large pool of youthful citizens, many tasks could be accomplished through the promotion of intergenerational relationships.

SOCIAL POLICY RECOMMENDATIONS

Despite the women's movement of the past two decades, or even two centuries, women still have not achieved social, economic, or legal equality. Indeed, apparently women's economic status has deteriorated over the past two decades (Stallard, Ehrenreich, and Sklar, 1983). For example, women's rights to obtain divorce did not deal with the patriarchal structure of marriage. Many have noted that women's economic status declines upon divorce.

Only recently has attention turned to the economic plight of women separated from their husbands by the process of institutionalization (McClory, 1988). Through a combination of awareness and creative economic policy the responsibility of social institutions can be developed to deal sensitively with the issues of older women.

Due to the longer life expectancy of females, social and economic issues become particularly salient for women as they age. "When old age became a social problem, women were left behind," as Rodeheaver

(1987) explains, the aging woman experiences no life course transition in her social welfare status that distinguishes her from younger women. Both have been disenfranchised from social policy by the assumption that their desired status is dependency on husbands. Policies are based on the implicit assumption of dependency, and the assumption that women's problems require private solution within the family.

This country has no national health policy (Kutza, 1981; Pegels, 1981). The passage of Title XVIII (Medicare) in 1965 and Title XIX (Medicaid) in 1967 provided new funding sources for long-term care institutions. Generally, Medicare pays for acute rather than chronic care. Once an institutionalized elderly person's assets are liquidated he/she becomes eligible for Medicaid. Seventy-five percent of nursing home patients in this country receive at least partial Medicaid support, which supplements their Social Security income to provide coverage for the cost of care (Crystal, 1982), which ranges between $1500 and $2600 per month. It has been estimated that 40% of the elderly in nursing homes use up their lifetime out-of-pocket savings within three months of placement (Branch, 1989).

Financial assistance payments directly to families who wish to keep older relatives at home is both humane and economically justifiable (Fengler and Goodrich, 1979; Linsk, Keigher, and Osterbusch, 1988). Butler (1977, 1978) feels that "if even a fraction of the sums used to support older people in nursing homes were available to help families provide for their elders, we would see a significant decrease in the number of those in institutions." In Sweden, tax-free payments of as much as $450 per month can be paid directly to a family that takes care of a chronically sick or handicapped person at home (Fengler and Goodrich, 1979). In the U.S., payments of up to $800 per month can be paid to family caregivers. Unfortunately, many families in this country are unaware of the availability of cash payments to family caregivers. Consumer education through newspapers, newsletters, the media, and adult education programs are a few suggestions for informing the public.

Although financial incentives for family caregivers have merit, the wives in this study provided a total of 182 years of personal in-home care to their husbands prior to placement and without financial assistance! The savings in cost of institutional care totals, conservatively, $3, 275,000. It was often mentioned by wives during the interview that home care had financial advantages over the astronomical cost of placement. Placement led to concerns about financial status.

The marketing of long-term care insurance has been impeded by inadequate data on cost. Another reason has to do with the inability to predict how many people would use such insurance. Perhaps another marketing problem is the public's aversion to plan for long-term care. Most wives in this study did not consider nursing home placement an acceptable substitute for the years they provided home care. Studies of placement issues should include inquiry regarding long-term care insurance. It is the researcher's speculation that the wives in this study would have resisted the notion of insurance as an added expense. It would he interesting to know how many couples had life insurance and whether both the insurance companies and the wives would be willing to use funds from insurance to cover the cost of long-term care. Criticisms of the social policies which directly affect long-term care are aimed at the lack of federal assistance for reimbursement. In order to change national, state and local restrictive policies, political pressure can be used to empower and mobilize people.

Information on the political issues which affect long-term care could be disseminated in a large print newsletter sent to families of nursing home residents. Newsletters have been a successful means of education and have been used by the Women's International League for Peace and Freedom, the Gray Panthers, and the American Association of Retired Persons. Gray America is growing older. Those over 65 comprise a significant body of constituents. Through advocacy and organization the older population can be helped to continue to use their political power effectively.

Successful organization designed to change social policy for the elderly can be carried out within and outside the nursing home. In Cambridge, Massachusetts, a social worker created a program centered on improving residents' rights (McDermott, 1989). Almost a decade ago in Minnesota, an advocacy initiative by community organizers, in conjunction with nursing home residents, brought about an increase in the state's monthly allotment to nursing home residents (Meyer, 1988).

National groups of organized elderly already exist and have resolved to win important legislative battles. Most recently, Congress passed the Medicare Catastrophic Protection Act. This act, which was controversial, contained provisions supported and won by the Gray Panthers, including a Medicare buy-in program and a prescription drugs benefit. In addition, allowable income of spouses of nursing home patients was raised to $786 per month by 1992. Assets increased to $12,000 beginning in 1992. Efforts to engage people, not just the elderly, to work toward progressive policies in long-term care will, in the end, reward us all.

The most obvious and glaring need to relieve the financial burden of long-term care is the legislative endorsement of Medicare reimbursement for nursing home placement. Another suggestion for policy makers would be to give a rebate or tax credit to those who have given care at home. Crisis placement and respite care could be arranged for those caregivers living with combative patients. Counter-arguments might propose that this type of legislation would promote abusive and neglectful caregivers in order to meet the criteria for special and expedient placement. In Canada, a new policy created by a life insurance company will allow AIDS patients who have paid into the program to withdraw their benefits before death in order to pay for in- home and institutional care (MacNeil-Lehrer Report, May 11, 1988). Such progressive policies and programs have applicability for the population reported on in this study.

Service allocations are determined by health care polices. Health care professionals and consumers must beware and be aware of existing social health policy, its ramifications, and creative alternatives for the future. As the aged population increases, the inadequacies of present policies become more apparent. The need for added reform in long-term care and health policy is urgent.

EDUCATION

Dissemination of information for and about the elderly and older women is possible by bringing the public's attention to the issues through political and community organizations, workshops, and literature and media campaigns.

The education of professionals in regard to the current research on the elderly and women occurs in journals of professional societies and conferences. However, clinicians who work in the field need in-service training. It is essential to have the support of an administrative staff, one that pursues opportunities designed to keep line staff informed, stimulated and challenged.

In nursing homes, adult day care centers, home health agencies, hospitals, senior and wellness centers, staff can benefit from presentations, videos, workshops, and shared materials such as books and articles, which offer new information, dispel myths, and encourage staff development and dialogue.

In the academic setting, gerontology and women's studies are the obvious avenues for the advancement and proliferation of the latest research and clinical wisdom. Other areas of study in the curriculum also offer opportunities to incorporate research and inform students on the issues of women and older people. It is a challenge to the academic professional to utilize progressive political material in support of a dialectic which inspires students and offers a different perspective.

RESEARCH RECOMMENDATIONS

Several questions have a high priority for future research:

1. How do the wives cope when they actually become widows: Do they blossom in relief or shrivel in despair? Does the "ongoing funeral" of nursing home placement help prepare the wife over time for the eventual separation from her husband by death?

A follow-up study which involves interviews with wives at time two (one year to eighteen months after initial interview) would identify those whose husbands had died. Their adjustment to actual widowhood could be compared with their adjustments when their husbands were in long-term care.

Ideally, a prospective, longitudinal study could be designed and implemented which would monitor pre-morbid, post-morbid, post-placement and post-mortem reactions of spouses to each situation. These data would reveal individual patterns of coping over time. Information about situational responses would be available as well.

2. Several studies suggest that older men may be less stressed and burdened by caregiving tasks than women, as men are more inclined toward the instrumental aspects of their relationships, as opposed to the emotional which characterize women (King, et al., 1986; , Zarit, Todd, and Zarit, 1986; Miller, 1987). In addition, as Neugarten and Gutmann

(1968) have proposed, men, as they age, seem to become more tolerant of their own nurturant and affiliative impulses.

Gender comparisons would be interesting to study, although it would be difficult to locate a sufficient sample of elderly men who had been caregivers and whose wives are institutionalized.

3.   In order to support the impression that age and time (history) are determinants of response to caregiving and the marriage, it is proposed that a control group of younger wives who have experienced the same event, long-term care of their husband, be studied in contrast to the sample of older wives. Over many years in a long-term marriage, spouses develop rationalizations about their relationships and behavior which gives meaning to their lives. A younger cohort has not had the time to build and reinforce such rationalizations and may perceive their caregiving role in less idealized terms. Furthermore, younger women may have more opportunities for economic freedom from their spouse. They are also living in a time when divorce is socially acceptable.

4.   Because all of the respondents in the study were Caucasian, it is important to explore differences or similarities in response among minorities. Comparing results of the instruments with Black and Hispanic elderly would yield cross-cultural data.

5.   Due to the epidemic rise in the number of persons with AIDS, demands on their caregivers have also risen dramatically. What distinguishes AIDS caregivers from caregivers of the elderly? How do their needs overlap? A comparative study could examine any correlates and propose recommendations for service delivery and policy.

Research development and evaluation of programs and clinical issues demand that researchers work closely with clinicians to initiate, fund, and promote the most appropriate services -- those that respond to the genuine needs of older people.

FEMINIST RESEARCHERS

Many traditional social scientists believe that the collection of data and its application are two distinct enterprises. In contrast, feminist researchers collect data with the explicit purpose of improving the lives of women and changing the status quo. What most distinguishes feminist researchers from more mainstream researchers is the feminist belief that data collection, its interpretation, and its use are all inherently political activities (Bograd, 1988). It is hoped that this research and list of recommendations will impact in a positive way on social change by addressing the prevention of elderly abuse through identification of a high risk group, by advocating for creative policy and program changes, and through clinical intervention and education.

IMPLICATIONS FOR THE FUTURE

Will the issues for older people be the same in years to come? Will wives still have the same commitment? It is possible that future generations of spouses will not make the personal sacrifices of the women in this study. Trends indicate increased long-term employment of women, a continued breakdown in family institutions such as traditional marriage, lack of commitment to traditional religions, eroding confidence in the medical profession, retracted health care and social security benefits.

The nature of the elderly's health care needs and their rate of utilizing health services is shifting the balance of health care from acute to chronic care. A lack of response from the government regarding reimbursement for long-term care, as well as the lack of support for a National Health Service policy, continue to negatively impact on the health care system.

Some interesting speculations can be offered:

1) The need and demand for long-term care will continue to grow;

2) The definition of chronological aging, for cultural and policy purposes, will be redefined upwards;

3) The political power of the elderly will expand, commensurate with their increased numbers;

4) The differential plight of women will not change if their longer   life expectancy continues.

The implications are both bleak and inspiring. The challenge lies in reforming policy and creating interventions that identify and address a vulnerable group of elderly women.

Appendices

Appendix A

Dear Mrs.

As a hospital social worker for ten years, I have been involved with hundreds of nursing home placements. Families who deal with this difficult decision have special issues, both financial and emotional. Very little has been written about the experience from the perspective of the wife who remains in the community once her husband has been placed. A careful study is needed to understand the meaning of the experience and to determine the needs of those like yourself.

Since your husband has been admitted for nursing home care, I would like to request your help in conducting my study. I would like your help to provide a one hour interview that can be conducted at a time and place convenient to you. Your name and other identifying information will not be used. Your comments will be confidential. Participation is voluntary and fully endorsed by the nursing home. If you do not wish to participate, it will not affect your husband's care in any way.

I will call you soon to confirm that you have received this letter and to answer any questions.

I look forward to talking with you.

Sincerely,

Maria C. Bartlett, M.A.

Appendix B

CONSENT FORM

" The purpose of the study in which I agree to participate is to understand how nursing home placement affects wives once their husbands become residents. My participation would involve answering several questionnaires, which will take approximately one hour.

My name and other identifying information will not appear or be used in the study. The information that I share will in no way jeopardize my husband's situation in the home. My comments will be held in confidence.

I understand that I can choose not to answer any questions. Participation is totally voluntary.

I have read and understand the information above and have received a copy of this form. I have volunteered to participate based on this information.

_____
Signature

_____
Date

Appendix C

QUESTIONNAIRE
* 1. How long in Nursing Home?
* 2. Any other Nursing Home?
* 3. Is he a veteran?
  4. How long have you been married?
  5. How would you describe your marriage before your husband became ill?
  6. How would you describe your marriage before your husband was placed in a nursing home?
  7. Would you say your marriage is affectionate?
  8. How did you resolve conflicts?
  9. Were you the person caring for your husband at home before he came to the nursing home? If so, how would you categorize your caregiving involvement?

> Duty/Obligation
> Love
> Reciprocity
> Guilt
> No One Else

10. Tell me about the burdens of caring for him at home.
11. Tell me about the benefits.
12. Would you say that the decision to place your husband was made in a time of crisis, or do you feel you had time to prepare for this change?
13. Did you feel you were in control of this decision? Why or why not?
14. What events led up to the decision to place your husband in a nursing home?
15. If couple has children, how did they help or hinder in your decision?
16. How much time do you spend with your family?

*Indicates addition to questionnaire as of 6-6-88, after 6 interviews.
**Indicates additions after 1-20-89.

Appendix C (continued)

17. How do you spend this time together?
18. How much time do you spend with friends?
19. How do you spend this time together?
20. Does religion play a significant part in your life? If so, how actively do you participate in church activities?
21. Are you in a support group?
*   21a.Do you have anyone to confide in?
22. Where have you found the most support during this transition?
23. Have any of the following happened to you this year?
    Change of residence
    Loss of a friend or relative
    Accident or change in health status
    Retirement
    Change in income
*   24. How were you and your husband affected by retirement?
*   25. Has your husband ever abused you verbally or physically?
** 25a.How often? Under what circumstances?
** 25b.Did you ever strike back?
*   26. Have you ever thought of divorce?
27. What did "nursing home placement" mean to you before your husband became ill?
28. What does it mean to you now?
29. What are the problems of having placed your husband in a nursing home?
30. What are the benefits?
31. How often are you able to visit? If "not often", what are the constraints?
32. How satisfied are you with these visits?
33. How satisfied are you with the care your husband receives in the nursing home?

Appendix C (continued)

34. What help do you provide for your husband in the nursing home?
35. Do you continue to feel like his primary helper, or do you feel more like a visitor in the nursing home? Why?
** 35a.What does marriage mean to you?
** 35b.Do you feel you have adjusted to the placement?
** 35c.If so, how have you managed to adjust?
36. How would you describe your marital relationship now?
37. How has your role as wife changed?
38. What is missing the most about your relationship?
39. What new problems have occurred for you as a result of your husband being in a nursing home?
** 39a.If you weren't caregiving for your husband, how would you spend your time?
* 40. How has the nursing home placement affected you financially?
* 41.How has the nursing home placement affected you emotionally?
42. How do you cope with change?
43. Is this the way you have always coped with change?
* 44. Does it help to help others?
45. How do you feel about the future in terms of yourself, your husband, and your marriage?
46. What would be of most help to you now?
** 47. What would have made a difference?
** 48. Do you have any advice for other women?
49. Is there anything you would like to add?

Appendix D

1. Circle the dot on the scale line below which best describes the degree of happiness, everything considered, of your marriage before the placement of your spouse. The middle point, "happy", represents the degree of happiness which most people get from marriage, and the scale gradually ranges on one side to those few who are very unhappy in marriage, and on the other, to those few who experience extreme joy or happiness in marriage.

0	2	7	15	20	25	35

Very Unhappy	Happy	Perfectly Happy

Check what corresponds to the appropriate extent of agreement or disagreement that exists between you and your spouse on the following items.

	Almost Always Agreed	Occasionally Disagreed	Frequently Disagreed	Almost Always Disagreed
2. Handling Family Finances				
3. Matters of Recreation				
4. Demonstrations of Affection				
5. Friends				
6. Sex Relations				
7. Conventionality (right, good or proper conduct)				
8. Philosophy of Life				
9. Ways of dealing with in-laws				

Appendix D (continued)

Please check the blank following the appropriate answer.

10. When disagreements arose they usually resulted in:
    My spouse giving in   _____
    My giving in   _____
    Agreement by mutual give and take   _____

11. Did you and your spouse engage in outside interests together?
    All of them   _____
    Some of them   _____
    Very few of them   _____
    None of them   _____

12. In leisure time did you generally prefer:
    To be "on the go"?   _____
    To stay at home?   _____

    Did your mate generally prefer:
    To be "on the go"?   _____
    To stay at home?   _____

13. Did you ever wish you had not married?
    Frequently   _____
    Occasionally   _____
    Rarely
    Never   _____

14. If you had your life to live over, do you think you would:
    Marry the same person   _____
    Marry a different person   _____
    Not marry at all   _____

15. Did you confide in your mate:
    Almost never   _____
    Rarely   _____
    In most things   _____
    In everything   _____

Apendix E

Below is a list of ways you might have felt or behaved. Please circle how often you have felt this way during the past week.

	Rarely or none of the time (less than 1 day) Cirlce 0	Some or a little of the time (1 -2 days) Cirlce 1	Occasion-ally or a moderate amount of the time (3-4 days) Cirlce 2	Most or all of the time (5-7 days) Cirlce 3
During the past week:				
1. I was bothered by things usually don't bother me.	0	1	2	3
2. I did not feel like eating; my appetite was poor.	0	1	2	3
3. I felt that I could not shake off the blues even with help from my family and friends.	0	1	2	3
4. I felt that I was just as good as other people.	0	1	2	3
5. I had trouble keeping my mind on what I was doing.	0	1	2	3
6. I felt depressed	0	1	2	3
7. I felt that everything that I did was an effort.	0	1	2	3
8. I felt hopeful about the future.	0	1	2	3
9. I thought my life had been a failure.	0	1	2	3
10. I felt fearful.	0	1	2	3
11. My sleep was restless.	0	1	2	3
12. I was happy.	0	1	2	3
13. I talked less than usual.	0	1	2	3
14. I felt lonely.	0	1	2	3
15. People were unfriendly	0	1	2	3
16. I enjoyed life.	0	1	2	3
17. I had crying spells.	0	1	2	3
18. I felt sad.	0	1	2	3
19. I felt that people dislike me.	0	1	2	3
20. I could not get "going".	0	1	2	3

Appendix F

Below are five pairs of circles. imagine that the large circle represents your husband and the small circle represents you. The more of the small circle that is inside the large circle, the closer you feel to your husband. Which pair best represents the situation for the two of you before he became ill?

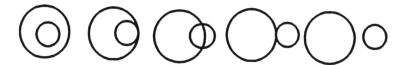

Below are five pairs of circles. imagine that the large circle represents your husband and the small circle represents you. The more of the small circle that is inside the large circle, the closer you feel to your husband. Which pair best represents the situation for the two of you before he became ill?

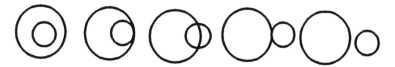

Appendix G

HEALTH OF WIFE

1. Do you have any chronic medical condition? Acute?
2. Have you visited the doctor in the last six months? If yes, why?
3. Do you take medications? If yes, what are they?
4. How would you rate your health prior to your husband's illness?
   Poor   Fair   Good   Excellent

5. How would you describe your physical health?
   Poor   Fair   Good   Excellent

HEALTH OF HUSBAND
1. What is your husband's illness?
2. Are your husband's impairments mostly physical, mental, or both?
3. How long has he been sick?
4. Is your husband bedridden?
5. Does he have control of his bowel and bladder?
6. Are the two of you able to communicate as you were before your husband became ill?
7. If he is unable to communicate with you, is there anyone else with whom he is able to be understood?

* 8. Do you feel you communicate on any level, physically, spiritually, or other?

* Indicates addition to questionnaire as of 6-6-88, after 6 interviews.

Appendix H

PERSONAL BACKGROUND/DEMOGRAPHICS

1. Race

   White, Non-Hispanic 1

   Black, Non-Hispanic . . . . 2 _____

   Hispanic 3   1

   Other (Specify) 4

2. Date of Birth_ _____ _____

                                                    2

3. Do you live alone?

   Yes . . . . 1 _____

   No 2   3

4. If you live with others, please specify their
   relationship to you.   _____

   Other (specify)_____   4

5. How much formal education do you have?

   One through 8 years 1

   Incomplete High School 2

   High School Completed 3

   Technical School 4

   Some College (1 - 3 years) . . . . 5 _____

   College Graduate 6   5

   Post-Graduate Study 7

6. What is your religious affiliation?

   Catholic 1

   Jewish . . . . 2 _____

   Protestant 3   6

   Other (specify) 4

APPENDIX H (continued)

7. Do you currently practice your religion?
    Yes 1
    No 2   7

8. Are you presently:
    Employed Full-Time 1
    Employed Part-Time 2
    Retired 3
    Disabled 4   8
    Homemaker 5
    Temporarily Unemployed 6

9. If you work, what is your occupation?

    _____

10. What is your annual income?
    Below $5,000 1
    $ 5,000 - $10,000 2
    $10,000 - $15,000 3
    $15,000 - $20,000 4   10
    Above $20,000 5

11. What was your highest annual income?
    Below $5,000 1
    $ 5,000 - $10,000 2
    $10,000 - $15,000 3
    $15,000 - $20,000 4   11
    Above $20,000 5

12. Is your income adequate or inadequate?
    Adequate 1
    Inadequate 2   12

CITED LITERATURE

Anderson, S., Russell, C., and Schumm, W.: Perceived marital quality of family life-cycle categories: A further analysis. Journal of Marriage and the Family, 45: 127-139, 1983.

Arkin, A.: Notes on anticipatory grief. In Anticipatory Grief, eds. B. Schoenberg, A.C. Carr, A.H. Kutscher, D. Peretz, and I.K. Goldberg, pp. 9-13. New York, Columbia University Press, 1974.

Ball, I.: Widow's grief: The impact of age and mode of death. Omega, 7: 307-333, 1977.

Bandura, A.: Self-efficacy mechanism in human agency. American Psychologist, 37: 122-147, 1982.

Bandura, A., Adams, N., and Beyer, I.: Cognitive processes mediating behavioral change. Journal of Personality and Social Psychology, 35: 125-139, 1977.

Bartlett, M.: What happens to the patients after nursing home placements? Paper presented at the Annual Coneference of the Association of Hospital Social Work Direcitors, St. Louis, MO., April, 1989.

Baum, M., and Baum, R.: Growing Old. Englewood Cliffs, NJ, Pentice Hall, Inc., 1980.

Beam, W.: College students' perceptions of family strengths. In Building Family Strengths, eds. N. Stinnett, B. Chesser, and J. DeFrain, pp. 31-37. Lincoln, NE, University of Nebraska Press, 1979.

Berg, S., Mellstrom, D., Persson, G., and Svanborg, A.: Loneliness in the Swedish aged. Journal of Gerontology, 36: 342-349, 1981.

Birren, I., Butler, R., Greenhouse, 5., Sokoloff, L., and Yarrow, M.: Human Aging (U.S. Public Health Service Publication No. 986). Washington, DC, U.S. Government Printing Office, 1963.

Blau, Z.: Old age in a changing society. New York: New Viewpoints. (abstract) 1973.

Blazer, D., Hughes, D., and George, L.: The epidemiology of depression in an elderly community population. The Gerontologist, 27: 281-286, 1987.

Block, M., & Sinnott, J. The Battered Elder Syndrome. Unpublished manuscript, Center on Aging, College Park, MD, 1979.

Bogdan, R.C., and Biklen, S.K.: Qualitative Research in Education. Boston, Allyn and Bacon, 1982.

Bograd, M.: Feminist perspectives on wife abuse: An introduction. In Feminist Perspectives on Wife Abuse, eds. K. Yllo and M. Bograd, pp. 11-26. Newbury Park, CA, SAGE Publications, Inc., 1988.

Borson, S., Barnes, R., Kukull, W., Okimoto, I., Veith, R., Inui, T., Carter, W., and Raskind, M.: Symptomatic depression in elderly medical outpatients I: Prevalence, demography, and health service utilization. Journal of the American Geriatrics Society, 34: 341-347, 1986.

Borys, S., and Perlman, D.: Gender differences in loneliness. Personality and Social Psychology Bulletin, 11: 63-74, 1985.

Bosse, R., Aldwin, C. Ekerdt, D., Levenson, M., & Workman-Daniels,K. How stressful is retirement? Manuscript submitted for publication, 1988.

Branch, L. Family care: Research and policy agendas for the 1990's. Keynote address, Michigan State University, East Lansing. March, 1989.

Breed, W.: Suicide and loss in social interaction. In Essays in Self Destruction, ed. E. Schnerdman. New York, Science House, 1967.

Brody, E.: Parent care as a normative family stress. The Gerontologist, 25: 19-29, 1985.

Burgess, E.W., and Cottrell, L.: Predicting Success or Failure in Marriage. New York, Prentice Hall, 1939.

Butler, R.: Nursing home care: An impossible situation unless. International Journal of Aging and Human Development, 8: 291-294, 1977-1978.

Callahan, J.: Elder abuse: Some questions for policy makers. The Gerontologist, 28: 453-458, 1988.

Creecy, R., Berg, W., and Wright, R.: Loneliness among the elderly: A causal approach. Journal of Gerontology, 40: 487- 493, 1985.

Crystal, S.: America's Old Age Crisis - Public Policy and the Two Worlds of Aging. New York, Basic Books, 1982.

Cuber, J., and Harroff, P.: The Sigificant Americans. New York, Appleton-Century-Crofts, 1965.

Dixon, S., and Sands, R.: Identity and the experience of crisis. Social Casework, April: 223-230, 1983.

Douglas, R., Hickey, T., and Noel, C.: A Study of Maltreatment of the Elderly and Other Vulnerable Adults. Institute of Gerontology, University of Michigan, Ann Arbor, MI, 1980.

Dressler, D. Life adjustment of retired couples. International Journal of Aging and Human Development, 4: 375-349, 1973.

Family Research Laboratory. Elder abuse and neglect: Recommendations from the research conference on elder abuse and neglect. Unpublished manuscript, University of New Hampshire, Durham, NH, 1986.

Fengler, A., and Goodrich, N.: Wives of elderly disabled men: The hidden patients. The Gerontologist, 19 175-183, 1979.

Finklehor, D.: Common features of family abuse. In The Dark Side of Families: Current Family Violence Research, eds. D. Finklehor, R. Gelles, G. Hotaling, and M. Straus, pp. 17-28. Beverly Hills, CA, SAGE Publications, 1983.

Finney, J., Moos, R., Cronkite, R., and Gamble, W. A conceptual model of the functioning of married persons with impaired partners: Spouses of alcoholic patients. Journal of Marriage and the Family, 45: 23-24, 1983.

Flaherty, J., Richman, J., Hozkinson, K., & Frank, E. Social zeitgeist and bereavement in widows. Paper presented at the Annual Meeting of the American Psychiatric Association, May, 1987.

Freud, S. Mourning and melancholia. In The Standard Edition of the Complete Psychological Works of Sigmund Freud. (Vol. 14). London, Hogart, 1957. (Original work published in 1917).

Fromm-Reichmann, F.: Loneliness. Psychiatry, 22: 1-15, 1959.

Gilford, R., and Bengston, V.: Measuring marital satisfaction in three generations: Positive and negative dimensions. Journal of Marriage and the Family, 41: 387-398, 1979.

Gilligan, C.: In a Different Voice. Cambridge, MA, Harvard University Press, 1982.

Gioglio, G., & Blakemore, P. Elder abuse in New Jersey: The knowledge and experience of abuse among older New Jerseyans. Unpublished manuscript, New Jersey Division on Aging, Trenton, NJ, 1983.

Giordano, N. Individual and family correlates of elder abuse. Unpublished doctoral dissertation, University of Georgia, 1982.

Given, B., Collins, C., & King, S. Predictors of caregiver's decision to institutionalize elderly family members. Symposium conducted at the Family Care: Research and Policy Agendas for the 1990's, East Lansing, March, 1989.

Goldman, S.: Social aging, disorganization, and the loss of choice. The Gerontologist, 11: 158-162, 1971.

Golodetz, A., Evans, R., Heinritz, G., and Gibson, C.: The care of chronic illness: The "responsor" role. Medical Care, 7: 385-394, 1969.

Gove, W., and Tudor, J.: Adult sex roles and mental illness. American Journal of Sociology, 78, 312-335, 1973.

Hageboeck, H., and Brandt, K.: A Summary Report of Rural/Urban Abuse of the Elderly in Scott County, Iowa: Iowa Gerontology Model Proiect. Iowa City, University of Iowa, 1981.

Hamilton, G.V.: A Research in Marriage. New York, Albert and Charles Boni, 1929.

Hammen, C., and Padesky, C.: Sex differences in the expression of depressive responses on the Beck Depression Inventory. Journal of Abnormal Psychology, 86: 609-614, 1977.

Hickey, T., and Douglas, R.: Mistreatment of the elderly in the domestic setting: An exploratory study. American Journal of Public Health, 71: 500-507, 1981.

Hill, C.D., Thompson, L.W., and Gallagher, D.: The role of anticipatory bereavement in older women's adjustment to widowhood. The Gerontologist, 28: 792-796, 1988.

Hill, E., and Dorfman, L.: Reactions of housewives to the retirement if their husbands. Family Relations, 31: 195-200, 1982.

Hinton, R.W.: Organizational socialization: Predictors of commitment during and after entry Doctoral dissertation, Northwestern University, Evanston, IL, 1981.

Holahan, C.K., and Holahan, C.J.: Self-efficacy, social support, and depression in aging: A longitudinal analysis. Journal of Gerontology, 42: 65-68, 1987.

Hudson,M.:Elder mistreatment: Current research. In Elder Abuse: Conflict in the Family, eds. K. Pillemer and R. Wolf, pp. 125-161. Dover, MA, Auburn House, 1986.

Johnson, C.L.: The impact of illness on late-life marriages. Journal of Marriage and the Family, 47(1): 165-172, 1985.

Keating, N., and Cole, P.: What do I do with him 24 hours a Day? Changes in the housewife role after retirement. The Gerontolorist, 20: 84-89, 1980.

King, S., Cornwell, K., Given, B., and Given, C.W.: Survey based on case studies of family caregivers. Paper presented at 39th Annual Meeting of the Gerontological Society of America, Chicago, Il., October, 1986.

Klein, R., Dean, A., and Bogdonof, M.: The impact of illness upon the spouse. Journal of Chronic Diseases, 20: 241-248, 1967.

Kosberg, J.: Preventing elder abuse: Identification of high risk factors prior to placement decisions. The Gerontologist, 28: 43-50, 1988.

Kutza, E.: The Benefits of Old Age - Social Welfare Policy. Chicago, University of Chicago Press, 1981.

Larson, R., Zuzanek, J., and Mannell, R.: Being alone versus being with people: Disengagement in the daily experience of older adults. Journal of Gerontology, 40: 375-381, 1985.

Lau, E., and Kosberg, J.: Abuse of the elderly by informal care providers.Aging, 299: 10-15, 1979.

Lewis, R.A., and Spanier, G.B.: Theorizing about the quality and stability of marriage. In Contemporary Theories about the Family (Vol. 2), eds. W.R. Burr, R. Hill, F.I. Nye, and I.L. Reiss, pp. 268-294. New York, The Free Press, 1979.

Linsk, N., Keigher, S., and Osterbusch, S.: State policies regarding paid family caregiving. The Gerontologist, 28: 204212, 1988.

Locke, H.J., and Wallace, K.M.: Short marital-adjustment and prediction tests: Their reliability and validity. Marriage and Family Living, August: 251-255, 1959.

Lofland, J.: Analyzing Social Settings. Belmont, CA, Wadsworth Publishing Company, 1971.

Lopata, H.Z.: Women's family roles in life course perspective. In Analyzing Gender, eds. B.B.Hess and M.M. Ferree, pp. 381-407. Newbury Park, CA, SAGE Publications, Inc., 1987.

McClory, R.: Growing old with Grace. The Reader, July 22: pp. 8-9, 26-29, 1988.

McDermott, C.: Empowering the elderly nursing home resident: The resident rights campaign. Social Work, March: 155-157, 1989.

MacKinnon, R., MacKinnon, C., and Franken, M.: Family strengths in long-term marriages. Lifestyles: A Journal of Changing Patterns, 1: 115-126, 1984.

MacNeil, R. and Lehrer, J. (co-producers). Special Report-Conversation with Jacquelyn Jackson-Quinn. [Television transcript] New york: WNET, November 1, 1988.

Matthiesen, V.: Adult Daughter's relationship with their institutionalized mothers. Unpublished doctoral disseertation, Rush University, Chicago, IL., 1986.

Meyer, M. Political organization of the institutionalized elderly. Paper presented at the Annual Meeting of the Gerontological Society of America, San Francisco, CA., November, 1988.

Middleman, R.: Role of perception and cognition in change. In Handbook of Clinical Social Work eds. A. Rosenblatt and D. Waldfogel, pp. 229-251. San Francisco, CA, Jossey-Bass, 1983.

Miles, M., and Huberman, A.M.: Qualitative Data Analysis. Beverly Hills, CA, SAGE Publications, Inc, 1984.

Miller, B.: Gender and control among spouses of the cognitively impaired. The Gerontologist, 27: 447-453, 1987.

Mitchell, R., Cronkite, R., and Moos, R.: Stress, coping and depression among married couples. Journal of Abnormal Psychology, 92: 433-448, 1983.

Moss, F., and Halmandaris, V.: Too Old, Too Sick, Too Bad. Germantown, MD, Aspen Systems Corp., 1977.

Neugarten, B.: Adult Personality: Towards a psychology of the life cycle. In Middle Age and Aging , ed. B. Neugarten, pp. 137-147. Chicago, University of Chicago Press, 1968.

Neugarten, B.: Personality and aging. In Handbook of the Psychology of Aging, eds. J. Birren and K.W. Schaie, pp. 626-649. New York, Van Nostrand Reinhold, 1977.

Neugarten, B., and Gutmann, D.: Age - sex roles and personality in middle age: A thematic apperception study. In Middle Age and Aging, ed. B. Neugarten, pp. 58-71. Chicago, University of Chicago Press, 1968.

O'Malley, H., Segel, H., and Perez, R.: Elder Abuse in Massachusetts: A Survey of Professionals and Paraprofessionals. Boston, Legal Research and Services for the Elderly, 1979.

O'Malley, T., Everitt, D., O'Malley, H., and Campion, E.: Identifying and preventing family mediated abuse and neglect of elderly persons. Annals of Internal Medicine, 98: 998-1005, 1983.

O'Rourke, M.: Elder Abuse: State of the Art. Boston, Legal Research and Services for the Elderly, 1980.

Parkes, C.: Recent bereavement as a cause of mental illness. British Journal of Psychiatry, 110: 198-204, 1964.

Payne, E.: Depression and suicide. In Modern Perspectives in the Psychiatry of Old Age, ed. J. Horvells, pp. 290-312. New York, Brunner-Mazel, 1975.

Pegels, C.: Health Care and the Elderly. Rockville, MD, Aspen Systems Corp., 1981.

Peplau, L., Russell, D., and Helm, M.: An attributional analysis of loneliness. In Attribution Theory: Application to Social Problems, eds. I.H. Frieze, D. Bar-Tal, and J.S. Carroll. New York, Jossey-Bass, 1979.

Perlman, D., and Peplau, L.: Toward a social psychology of loneliness. In Personal Relationships 3: Personal Relationships in Disorder, eds. S. Duck and R. Gilmour, pp. 31-56. London, Academic Press, 1981.

Perlman, H.H.: Persona. Chicago, University of Chicago Press, 1968.

Pillemer, K.: The dangers of dependency: New findings on domestic violence against the elderly. Social Problems, 33: 146-158, 1985.

Pillemer, K., and Finklehor, D.: The prevalence of elder abuse: A random survey. The Gerontologist, 28: 51-57, 1988.

Pineo, P.: Disenchantment in the later years of marriage. Marriage and Family Living, 23: 3-11, 1961.

Qualls, S., Norfleet, D., & Harder, E. Loneliness in spousal caregivers of the intellectually and physically impaired aging. Paper presented at the annual meeting of the Gerontological Society of America, Chicago, IL., November, 1986.

Radloff, L.S.: The CES-D scale: A self-report depression scale for research in the general population. Applied Psychological Measurement, 3:385-401,1977.

Reichard, S., Livson, F., and Peterson, P.: Aging and Personality. New York, Wiley, 1962.

Richman, J., and Flaherty, J.: Coping and depression: The relative contribution of internal and external resources during a life cycle transition. Journal of Nervous and Mental Disease, 173: 590-595, 1985.

Rodeheaver, P.: When old age became a social problem, women were left behind. The Gerontologist, 27: 741-745, 1987.

Rollins, B., and Feldman, H.: Marital satisfaction over the family life cycle. Journal of Marriage and the Family, 32: 20- 28, 1970.

Russell, D., Peplau, L., and Cutrona, C.: The revised UCLA loneliness scale: Concurrent and discriminant validity evidence. Journal of Personality and Social Psychology, 39: 472-480, 1980.

Silverman, P.R.: Widow to Widow. New York, Springer Publishing Company, Inc., 1986.

Snyder, D.K.: Multidimensional assessment of marital satisfaction. Journal of Marriage and the Family, November: 813-823, 1979.

Srole, L., and Fischer, A.: The Midtown Manhattan Longitudinal Study vs. "The Mental Paradise Lost" doctrine. Archives of General Psychiatry, 37: 209-221, 1980.

Stallard, K., Ehrenreich, B., and Sklar, H.: Poverty in the American Dream: Women and Children First. Boston, South End, 1983.

Steurer, J., and Austin, E.: Family abuse of the elderly. Journal of the American Geriatric Society, 28: 372-376, 1980.

Stinnett, N., Sanders, G., DeFrain, J., and Parkhurst, A.: A nationwide study of families who perceive themselves as strong. Family Perspective, 16: 15-22, 1982.

Stinnett, N., and Sauer, K.: Relationship characteristics of strong families. Family Perspective, 11: 3-11, 1977.

Stokes, J., and Levin, I.: Gender differences in predicting loneliness from social network characteristics. Journal of Personality and Social Psychology, 51: 1069-1074,1986.

Stommel, M., Given, C., & Given, B. Depression as in overriding variable explaining caregiver burden. Paper presented at the annual meeting of The Gerontological Society of America, San Francisco, CA., November, 1988.

Straus, M.: Measuring intrafamily conflict and violence: The Conflict Tactics (CT) Scales. Journal of Marriage and the Family, 41: 75-88, 1979.

Straus, M.: Sexual inequality, cultural norms, and wife beating. Victimology, 1: 54-76, 1976.

Straus, M.: Wife-beating: How common, and why? Victimology, 2: 443-458, 1977.

Swenson, C., and Trahaug, G.: Commitment and the long-term marriage relationship. Journal of Marriage and the Family, November: 939-945, 1985.

Szinovacz, M.: Female retirement: Effects on spousal and marital adjustment. Journal of Family Issues, 1: 423-440, 1980.

Terman, L.M., and Oden, M.H.: The gifted child grows up, Vol. IV. In Genetic Studies of Genius, pp. 431-433. Palo Alto, Stanford University Press, 1947.

Townsend, P.: The Family Life of Old People. London, Routledge and Kegan Paul, 1957.

Turner, R.: Family Interaction. New York, Wiley, 1970.

Waltz, M.: Marital context and post-infarction quality of life: Is it social support or something more? Social Science Medicine, 22: 791-805, 1986.

Warren, C.A.B.: Gender issues in field research. In Qualitative Research Methods, Vol. 9. Newbury Park, CA, SAGE Publications, Inc., 1988.

Weisman, A.: Is mourning necessary? In Anticipatory Grief, eds. B. Schoenberg, A.C. Carr, A.H. Kutscher, D. Peretz, and I.K. Goldberg, pp. 14-18. New York, Columbia University Press, 1974.

Weiss, R.: The study of loneliness. In Loneliness: The Experience of Emotional and Social Isolation, ed. R.S. Weiss, pp. 19-29. Cambridge, MA, MIT Press, 1973.

White, R.: Strategies of adaptation: An attempt at systematic description. In Coping and Adaptation, eds. G. Coelho, D., Hamburg, and J. Adams, pp. 47-68. New York, Basic Books, 1974.

Wingard, D., Jones, D., and Kaplan, R.: Institutional care utilization by the elderly: A critical review. The Gerontologist, 27:156-163,1987.

Wiseman, JP.: The research web. Urban Life and Culture, 3: 317-328, 1974.

Wolf, R., Godkin, M., and Pillemer, K.: Elder Abuse and Neglect: Report from Three Model Projects. Worcester, MA, University of Massachusetts Medical Center, 1984.

Wolf, R., Godkin, M., and Pillemer, K. Maltreatment of the elderly: A comparative analysis. Pride Institute Journal of Long Term Home Care, 5: 10-17, 1986.

Zarit, 5., Todd, P., and Zarit, J.: Subjective burden of husbands and wives as caregivers: A longitudinal study. The Gerontologist, 26:260-266, 1986.

Zarit, S.H., Reever, K., and Bach-Peterson, J.: Relatives of the impaired elderly: Correlates of feelings of burden. The Gerontologist, 20: 649-655, 1980.

BIBLIOGRAPHY

Abramson, L., and Sackheim, H: A paradox in depression: Uncontrollability and self-blame. Psychological Bulletin, 84: 838-851, 1977.

Adams, R.: Patterns of network change: A longitudinal study of friendships of elderly women. The Gerontologist, 27: 222- 227, 1987.

Beck, A.: Depression: Clinical, Experimental and Theoretical Aspects. New York, Harper and Row, 1967.

Bernard, I.: The Future of Marriage. New York, World Publishing, 1972. Bernard, J.: The Future of Marriage. New Haven, CT, Yale University Press, 1982.Booth, R.: Toward an understanding of loneliness. Social Work, March-April: 116-119, 1983.

Burgess, E.W., and Wallin, P.: Engagement and Marriage. Philadelphia, J.B. Lippincott Company, 1953.

Davidson, G.: Living with Dying. Minneapolis, Augsburg Publishing House, 1975.

Richman, I., and Flaherty, J.: Sex differences in drinking among medical students: Patterns and psychosocial correlates. Journal of Studies on Alcohol, 47: 283-289, 1986.

Stinnett, N., Sanders, G., and DeFrain, I.: Strong families: A national study. In Family Strengths III, eds. N. Stinnett, J. DeFrain, K. King, P. Knaub, and G. Rowe, pp.33-4I. Lincoln, NE, University of Nebraska Press, 1981.

Swensen, C., and Trahaug, G.: Mental Problems of Older Married Couples. Bergen, Norway, Psychology Institute, University of Bergen, 1979.